NOW IT IS POSSIBLE TO BE
AT ONE WITH THE UNIVERSE

ceachings of the winged disk

The study of Hermetics is a quest for union with God. And the goal of spirituality is to evolve to a higher state and unite oneself with the God-force.

This unity can be achieved with High Magick. Magick makes one's life all that it should be. It for those who want to know more about their true selves, their potential and their purpose. Practitioners of the Magickal Path are in harmony with the universe—because the practice of white Magick is in accordance with all nature—and so find that events work with them instead of against them.

The teachings of the spiritual leader Phaedron∴, of the Holy Order of the Winged Disk, are based on magickal explanations of the Egyptian pantheon, the Qabalah, the tarot, and other ancient knowledge and practices compiled for the first time in this book. Now one can learn to tap into the divine energy of the cosmos.

The philosophy of Western Magick
and a spiritual path to attainment

TEACHINGS OF THE WINGED DISK

Phaedron∴

Hierophant, Holy Order of the Winged Disk

Teachings of the Winged Disk
Phaedron∴, Hierophant,
The Holy Order of the Winged Disk

ISBN: 0-9637498-3-8

First printing: January 1997

A division of Toad Hall, Inc.
Rural Route 2, Box 16 B
Laceyville, PA 18623

Dedication

Thank you to the Gods who have given us the creativity, knowledge, spirit, and excellent facilities to produce the pages of this book. On behalf of all the initiates and students of The Holy Order of The Winged Disk who worked hard and ingeniously to put this book together, as well as the G.H. Hierophant.

It took years of full-time work for this book to be produced properly in the magickal way. It is a testimonial and manifestation of what a body of true spiritual seekers can do. I. as G.H. Hierophant also had to attend to the full-time duties of my position at the same time! The enthusiasm, devotion, abilities, and love that I was surrounded by in this project were inspiring to say the least. No one doubted its outcome or asked for reward, as true seekers realize that a true magickal Order with true magickal goals (on many levels) is their vehicle for attaining to the summit of the Great Work. And, their obligation for this privilege is to give back in return (as their predecessors gave for them to partake of this opportunity), for others may desire this path. Each person truly deserved the opportunity to be a part of the Order's very important document. The challenge of coordinating this book belongs to my spiritual wife who perfectly observed and demonstrated to others the fine example of our Magick and our cause.

Blessings,

Phaedron ∴

G.H. Hierophant

Holy Order of The Winged Disk

table of contents

Part Three "In Practice"

Introduction

A Special Note to Every Reader

Consider life as a journey from birth through life into death. Consider also that this journey continues even beyond, earth, in one way or another.

The purpose of life is broadly: self-improvement; evolution; growth; preparation; reformation leading to a union with perfection in one form or another. Therefore everybody possesses a spiritual purpose, whether or not one practices a spiritual path. Spiritual does not mean religious, but "the person within and without." Eating, working, and playing are just as spiritual as ritual, prayer, and meditation since all are directed as fortifying the individual and its mirror, the soul. Of course destructive acts can inhibit the advancement of the individual and the soul. This book does not attempt to designate what acts are fulfilling or defeating; this is a personal experience.

A genuine course of spirituality gives you the key to hitherto unopened doors. It offers the individual components that when integrated successfully, form the whole of perfection. You cannot develop "intuition" without stilling the mind. You cannot read Tarot without intuition. Larn Qabalah and you will understand every tradition in the world, since each uses it! Understand the self and you will understand the universe. The greatest alchemists claim that the transmutation of lead into gold is a minute duplication of the cosmos, but it can't be achieved by anyone who does not know Creation (himself). You can't control the conditions of your life until you learn to control your self. A healthy body cannot exist with an unhealthy mind. A healthy mind cannot exist in illusion or with an unhealthy body.

Perfection is the expression of each individual's Will to the fullest extent possible, as dictated by his own nature. It is man's natural instinct to grow toward this complete state.

Spiritual growth requires guidance. Those few who have laboriously risen totally above life's circumstances are here to teach, not lead. They will never flaunt their attained state of humanity. Their humility is one of the reasons they became attained. At the same time, it is important not to consider people as inferior because of their lack of spiritual attainment. Just because some have a particular talent does not mean those who do not show it are worthless.

You'll read herein, that there are no morals or ethics in spiritual attainment. Such are set by cultures and times and differ so often that their inconsistencies are the form of mere philosophy and useless custom.

In short, there are age-old roots upon which every tradition was established. Scholars and holy men have generally agreed that there is one source from which all others sprang. Yet the origins of this one source are shrouded in myths of lost continents. So at a time when Gods and men walked the face of the earth together, there emerged the seed of every tradition to follow. It is the basis of this book. However, to idolize this or any of the many books of spiritual wisdom is foolish. Revel in it but do not memorize it!

This book teaches the heretofore hidden side of the occult, hidden because it is only taught by Masters. It is not complete. No book can be "the book." However, it is thorough without omitting the important part of the highest principles in spiritual learning. This book does, however, teach the methods in which one should approach Magick, since there are so many overlapping facets that must be grasped to get the whole. Everything in this book is interrelated, just as nature is so connected. You cannot specialize in just one area as if it were an isolated specific discipline.

Magick does not make sense. It just happens. If you understand God and Its precepts, you've missed the boat. True mystical experience goes beyond intellectual understanding! What difference does it make if you understand what just happened or not? There are many well-read Magickians out there who can explain any phenomenon, but they can never experience anything other than mere intellectual rationalization. Actually, the universe does not conform to man's comprehension of three-dimensional things.

Replace your desire to know "why" with a burning desire to simply experience that "why." After you've experienced it, admit that you cannot explain it, but instead you can revel in

In a world where everyone is offered "the answers," the seeker
is conditioned into believing in blind faith. Instead this book, by
offering you "the question," will teach much wisdom that can
provide you. These questions lead to your true knowledge and
are much more useful and satisfying. Everyone has the answers,
but no one offers the questions. Science has had the answers to
questions, such as the origin of the universe; the building of the
Great Pyramid; why people see strange lights in the sky; providing all sorts of information that will keep the overactive mind
stimulated and increase the support of its followers. The problem is that these answers change from decade to decade!

So life is spirituality. The teachings found in this book are
not new. They are the age-old foundation of Magick. This
book contains deeper, usable concepts that were formerly only
accessible to students of adepts, yet, the layperson and the experienced practitioner should read it the same. The college pro-
fessor can depend on it for his authority; the practitioner can
use it to enhance his practices; the curious can use it to answer
some questions about spirituality.

This book can be used by: a) those already on a spiritual path;
b) those who want to learn about Magick; c) those who suspect
that there may be more to spirituality than what they have to
show for their current system or belief. Since the teachings
found in this book are the foundation of *all* spiritual teachings,
it will obviously benefit participants of any faith.

Everyone on the spiritual journey of life should be taught
what is in this book. Some modern leaders don't possess
this knowledge. Those that do only dispense the details and procedures to their more advanced students so that the populace
won't harm themselves. But do not expect to find in this or any
book, the key or step-by-step directions to your own personal
enlightenment. It is an individual process. Such guidance can
only be granted to those who prove themselves capable to their
spiritual teacher. And everyone who desires to learn true spirituality needs a teacher, despite the movements that promote
"self-illumination." (They arise in every generation.)

For those searching for a path, this book will help them to understand many paths and perhaps choose one. This book will
supplement the knowledge you already have. However, know

that knowledge alone is useless without the wisdom and force to use it. That which you are meant to know at this time can be used as needed.

Be advised that this book is not the only authority on attainment, nor is this Western Hermetic path a coercive one. The teachings revealed herein center around no single person, God, dogma, or organization. All teachings have emanated from the One. If this is your path, don't assume it is everyone's path. Let those close to you know about it, but never distort their true Will by coercing them to read this book.

The knowledge imparted in this book is such that one who reads it becomes responsible not to abuse it. I have been prudent in not dispensing too much for the reader to appropriately handle. Read this book for information, or interest, but not for idle amusement.

In closing this introduction, I have selected one thought to leave you with. Although the following quote doesn't really encapsulate *The Teachings of the Winged Disk*, it captures some overall concepts and is relevant to the average reader on whom dogma is often forced.

It is from Hermes Trismegistus, elaborated upon by an occultist of the early 20th century and then commented upon by me.

> *"For a discourse upon the holiest matters of religion would be profaned by a too numerous audience. It is an impiety to deliver to the knowledge of a great number, a treatise full of divine majesty"*
>
> —Hermes Trismegistus
>
> *"It is the indiscriminate disclosure of spiritual mysteries to those who, by reason of their exclusively fleshy condition, are incapable of appreciating and receiving them, that is called by Jesus a casting of pearls before swine."*
>
> —Anna Kingsford (translator of the above)

The reader of this book is urged before he goes on any further, to reread the above quote and footnote, to understand it, and not let it escape into the wasteland of illusion and rationale.

Those leaders who profane their most reverent traditions are referred to here. They are the foolish, yet clever, impersonal propagators of their organizations, recruiting, proselytizing, and allowing anyone to buy their goods in the name of public relations. If this is what you have, please continue reading until the real thing comes along. It is certainly better than watching television or getting drunk. It will help you, entertain you, and may even inspire you. No man or woman should be without ethics. But if you desire spirituality made manifest where the worship produces spiritual change and growth, do not support any man or woman with your energy when you should be supporting God(s). For this, allow yourself to be open and your path shall find its way to you.

Notes

Occasionally in this book, you'll find the term, "The Great Work." This is the Magickian's quest for union with God. This broad term is derived from the alchemical meaning of finding the Philosophers Stone, which is synonymous with it.

Another term is "The Great White Brotherhood." This is the entirety of all genuine movements aimed at union with God. The "Great White Brotherhood" is not a formal organization but rather an umbrella of all occult groups. "White Magick" as used here means "positive" as opposed to "black" meaning evil. There are no racial implications whatsoever. In Magick, there is no racial (or any other group) superiority or inferiority. Such disputes were created by governments for their pawns. God knows no overall prejudices! The same goes for the word "Brotherhood," which does not mean only men! Such usage is "proper English," which admittedly leaves a lot to be desired.

Where "he" or "she" is used it should not be taken literally but pertains to both sexes. Neither god or goddess nor man or woman is superior. I must conform to a "standard grammatical criteria," although I, too, consider it often obsolete. Thus words such as "he" and "she" should be read and understood in that context.

No mortal gender allocation to God has been made. God is not limited to human restrictions. Thus God and the Goddess are generally called God here.

God is sometimes referred to as "Nature", "It", etc. There is no good comprehensive definition of God possible, so I use these labels. Disregard your terminology of God as a religion; nature as trees, animals and accidental occurrences of the universe; consider God superior to any animate object and not subject to the mortal characteristic of male or female. (In fact, God is the root from which both emanated.)

The terms "Spiritual Teacher," "Master," "Hierophant," are synonymous.

"Occult" is a term that means "secret or hidden." "Esoteric" means any phenomenon which is "invisible."

The term "Magick" in this work, means generally all esoteric forms of occultism, irregardless of a sect, group or other minute differentiation. "Occultist" refers to practitioners of all forms of esotericism, i.e. the mystic, Magickian, spiritualist, pagan, etc.

In some places in this book you'll find Magick referred to as a science and in other places an art. Which one is it? It is both; it acts as a science when you recognize phenomena caused by Magick. It acts as an art when you are creating phenomena.

PART ONE

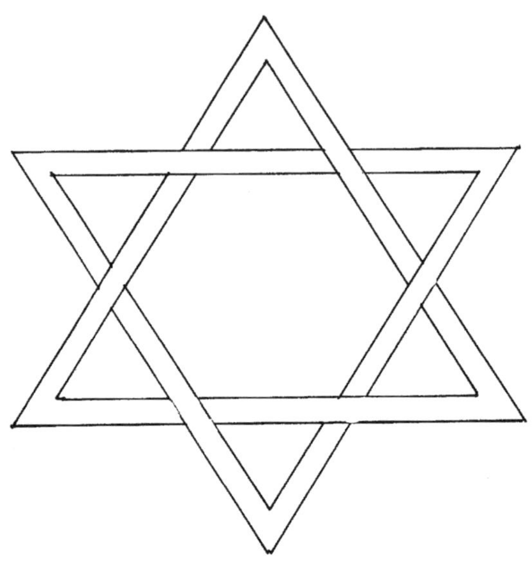

"The Groundwork"

Magick allows one to effect change in accordance withWill. It is the purpose of the Magickian to integrate his own higher self (and therefore that cosmic power that the higher self calls upon) with his own conscious self; this brings forth the life of the soul on an exoteric level. It should enhance his daily experiences.

This union (the higher with the lower) is represented by the six-pointed star of the ancient Egyptians, borrowed later by a few other traditions. It is simply two intertwined triangles; one upward representing the higher self; one downward representing the lower self. The hexogram symbolizes the attempt to bring into one's life that force which created oneself. It is ultimate unity.

What is Magick?

The study of Magick is Egyptian in origin. It is the oldest recorded path of spirituality. It is said to have been taught by the God Thoth at a time when "men and Gods walked the face of the Earth together." Thoth was later called Hermes by the Greeks, thus the name "Hermetic" evolved.

Over thousands of years, this tradition was repeatedly adapted to meet the changing states of man's development. Its mystical teachings formed the foundation of Gnosticism, Alchemy, Ritual Magick, Rosicrucianism and, most significantly, the mystical Qabalah; thus Hermetic is a very broad term.

One of the regular cyclical resurgences of Magick surfaced around the turn of the twentieth century. Great Magickal orders were founded. Magickal personalities such as Crowley, Mathers, Waite, Blavatsky, and Wescott made their marks that are still familiar to use today. One reason Aleister Crowley added a "k" to the word Magick was to differentiate this spiritual path from the common slight of hand that the word "magic" had become identified with. Yet, it should be clear that the wielding of Nature's forces did not originate there. Contrary to some enthusiasts, no one person or organization can lay claim to being the founder of Magick. In fact, the early precepts of Western Magick stress the obsolescence of worshipping any organization or person.

> *Change is stability.*

Practicing Magick in accordance with Nature is what this book is about and is commonly referred to as "white" Magick. It can also be called Western, Ceremonial, Hermetic, or Ritual Magick. Traditionally, since we consider all paths to have a Magickal base, it is not exclusive from *any* path. So it is common to find some Eastern, or non-ritual practices and principles employed. Whatever you call it, know that

Magick is the calling forth of natural forces using formulated methods, for the purpose of self development. The power of Magick lies in man's control over the elements, for fear and misunderstanding of the laws of Nature can lead to direct conflict with Nature/Creator/God.

Change is stability. If one of the planets failed to change its place within its own orbit, even for a second, the solar system would fail and be destroyed. When dinosaurs couldn't adapt to the climate changes in their environment they became extinct. The same has also occurred in the plant kingdom. When

Paracelsus here depicts the Magickian (Juggler) as wielding the forces of nature.

one person cannot adapt to changes in one's life, this maladjustment causes great distress and instability.

The Magickian learns to overcome the elements that could oppose his Will and happiness, for it has been so designed by the "Master Plan" that perfected man doesn't resist change but continues to exert his individuality to overcome adverse elements.

So Magick is the ability to cause change, and everyone performs magickal acts without even knowing it! The act of getting dressed in the morning is a transmutation from your consciousness to a final result. Cooking, reading, communicating, inducing sleep are some everyday examples of causing change. It is only when these changes seem profound that they are called Magick!

Even then, the standards change from time to time. Curing disease with penicillin would have been called Magick a few hundred years ago. Today it is called science. Plotting planetary movements or the earth's weather was once called Magick. A mere century ago, a "glowing house" (one that used electric lights) was emphatically called the "devil's work!"

Our science is referred to as High Magick. High is not a judgmental term; it means Magick calling forth the energy which produces the end result. Low Magick calls forth the end result. As an example, to make the Nile rise and irrigate their fields, the Egyptians practicing High Magick prayed to the God of the Nile. Those practicing Low Magick prayed to the Nile itself (or in a more modern example, if one wanted to sell a painting, one would pray to God that represents prosperity, not the painting itself).

All acts of creation are Magick. The line between science and Magick changes daily, but more important than these labels is the ability to control the self to the point of being able to cause desired change.

Since the purpose of Magick is to make one's life all that it should be (according to one's karmic birthright and Will), Magick is for those who want to know more about their "true" self and its potential and purpose. It is one way for those who want to realize their soul's purpose in this incarnation. It is for those who want to unite with their own perfect Will (i.e. Nature/Creator/God). Magick is not for those who believe they are only good enough to accept whatever crumbs fate gives them in this existence.

The way the artist of Magick learns is not very different from how one learns science or even simpler mechanics! The aspirant studies the principles and laws of Nature.[1] Astronomy now recognizes gravity, black holes, antimatter, ion rocket propulsion, and double (twin) stars, all of which were at one time thought to be scientifically impossible. Biologists have isolated

---

1. Nature as used here is not meant as trees, wind etc. Nature in the Magickal sense means all manifestation and non-manifestation as expressions of God/Creator.

previously unexplainable life-substances called DNA. Computer scientists use crystals in an electrical circuit to remember and calculate information for them. Horticulturists learned that by hooking up a polygraph to a leaf, they could record defensive and other plant reactions. Kirilian photographs give scientific evidence of an aura, the life force radiating from any organism, and even the "Magick" of DaVinci and others who invented "flying machines" is now commonly accepted as scientific fact. These are laws of Nature, called Magick! There are still many more phenomena that Magickians behold that science will uncover in the future and label "discoveries."

The ancients say man is on this planet because it is in accordance with his state of development at this time. Thus, man must learn via the human experience before perfection can be his. Qabalistically the Earth is related to Binah on the Tree of Life.

Thus man has unnatural ills. He is bound to a body of elements. The birth trauma is the greatest pain in life. He further has to endure the ills of the flesh, and the pain of the ego. He experiences separation from his Creator and must diligently struggle back to oneness with God.

> *If you do not make use of what you have been given, it may be taken away.*

Then man faces death, the second greatest trauma for most. His life-span is unnaturally short. Although some poets have described Earth as Hell, it is not, but it is certainly where man meets the taskmaster! Earth is the place where man learns through suffering.

To think that disease, heartbreak, ignorance, and oppression are necessary components of life is not the magickal way. It is not necessary to settle for these things or accept them as standards of living while believing that you are happy and complete. Thus, Magick!

Practitioners of the magickal path live in harmony with the universe and things cooperate with their Wills, instead of working against them. They are above inertia, and restriction will affect them less and less. Unfavorable events will bypass them.

Practicing Magick and doing one's Will serves the highest purpose by assisting Nature in Her work. This varies with the amount of commitment one wishes to make, for all are not intended to be Adepts.

The Magickian lives in a delightful place. He lives longer than most people, but is not immortal as some say, because all physical lives must eventually end, and to do otherwise would be against Nature. However, some Magickians, it is said, live for thousands of years.

The Magickian leads an ideal life and is never in need. He has so much control over his life and is so aligned with the forces of nature that those who don't understand call his achievements supernatural.

The Magickian learns and masters the lessons of life. His efforts allow him to express his own talents and to transform or discard whatever restricts his Will. He attracts joy and true luxury and overcomes the illusions of self-fabricated or material-based happiness. Through affecting his own Will, he knows personally what true happiness is; thus, he is free of frustrations and fears.

To summarize, the laws of Nature are what we harness for our own benefit. The whole world, including the plant and mineral kingdoms eventually benefit from each individual's growth. These laws can be learned through the study of Magick and each person can avert the problems and suffering that most people consider to be a part of life. It is not only every person's right to employ these tools but his obligation as well.

If you do not make use of what you have been given, it may be taken away. Each person is given a purpose along with a body (the vehicle) so he can pursue and implement his own perfection as an integral part of mankind.[2] To abuse that purpose or take it for granted is considered a great vice by the Magickian.

---

2. The Creator enabled you to inhabit your body as a vehicle carrying out your Will. Thus, the corporeal body cannot be regarded as evil. It is merely the condition that the soul must endure in order to incarnate and work on the earth plane.

What is the Occult?

"It is given to you to know the mystries."
—Jesus, Matthew 13:11

Typical human behavior fears that which is unknown, for example, entering a dark, unfamiliar room; beginning a new job; having a neighbor of another culture.

Occultism is the recognition of mysteries unexplainable by human intellect; such recognition exists in every human being. Anyone who believes in God is definitely an occultist![1] Yet if you ask the average person what the occult is, they probably either don't know or think it has something to do with Devil worship. The occult is misunderstood by most today, and it is thus feared. This fear occurs historically in cycles when esotericism becomes popular in a new or different form.

Acting on fear can be dangerous. Often we hear of a person unknowingly assaulting his or her mate who is entering the house late at night, fearing it them to be an attacker. Often, we read of whites attacking blacks or blacks attacking whites out of fear of not knowing another's life-style. Just the fear of suddenly passing a trailer truck on the highway has caused fatal accidents.

The healthy person overcomes fear by learning about it, then deciding if it is a threat to him or not. This decision can take place in as little as a second. In the unhealthy mind, the irrational and destructive reaction to fear causes the person to attack blindly.

Sociological studies show that fearful people band together in search of strength and to justify each other's fear or aggressions. This sociopathic behavior is dangerous when such a group attempts to wage war on the object of their fear. Their ignorance of managing fear can actually cause it to be self-directed—sort of a self-destruct mechanism of the deeper sub-

---

1. A broad term encompassing all of esotericism. It refers to the mystic Magickian, spiritualist, pagan, etc.

conscious. Thus, fear unchecked and driving, often becomes a "cancer" of the mind.

Should the occult be feared? Is it a threat? Is the occult only increasing among teenagers? Is it anti-religion? Is it practiced by perverts who claim their crimes come from the "word of God"?

There is no known conspiracy of any minority spiritual paths attacking any person, religious or governmental group. True, there will always be radical factions in society. They should not be generalized to religions, political or social movements. Excluding these few exceptions, let's examine what is "occult."

The transmutation of bread and wine from the "life force" of flesh and blood is occult. Certain divine communications invoked by way of a supernatural (i.e. magickal) experience that gave Moses divine information are occult. Jesus walking the face of the earth and performing alleged magickal acts is also occult. Even the sun rising this morning is occult. Transforming an idea or vision into tangible matter is an occult phenomenon. And when a bunch of laboratory-obtainable chemicals are combined in the same proportions as the human body but fail to come to life by themselves, this is an occult mystery!

> *Acting on fear can be dangerous.*

A true occultist recognizes spirit in everything. That means he uses the forces of Nature (as in the above examples) to make things happen. Most occultists are constructive and the end results of the operations will assist in their own self-improvement, and consequently their energy positively affects the world as a whole. They use the forces of nature in accordance with Nature's laws.

An occultist recognizes that it is no accident that there are nine planets, all the proper size, distance, and velocity, traveling on basically the same plane, all in the same direction. He understands this occurrence as having a deeper meaning. This and other syncronicities make it possible for the solar system to work precisely. One slight variation, for but a moment;

would cause an implosion, resulting in chaotic disarray and the system's collapse. The occultist believes that some Supreme Cosmic Agent must be behind such a mechanism. This agent is not comprehensible to human intellect.

Yesterday's Magick is today's science. Medicine, flying machines, atoms, a central sun not revolving around the earth, telepathy, computers, RNA/DNA, the telephone, etc. were all at one time considered sorcery or witchcraft. When man became familiar with them, his fear vanished and he declared them no longer occult but scientific. How vain! The occultist studies and uses subtle forces today that may be understood to the populace as tomorrow's science.

Fear the occult no more than you fear the automobile. Its operator can use this tool to make his life easier, or he can devastate or even kill with it. What you should fear is anyone who blindly uses power for his own vain, manipulative or unguided self-centeredness; he will employ them at anyone's expense, fear-followers of blatant destructive ideas. These ideas can be formed through physical intellectual, subliminal, or universal means. Fear too, the blind-faith followers who subordinate their Will to an organization, book, idea, person, or religion.

When you read about fanatics who call themselves occultists, know that they are frauds. They are the obscure "rebels of Nature" not trained by anyone, but usually out of control individuals with psychotic tendencies.

The Will

"Do what thou wilt shall be the whole of the Law.
Love is the Law. Love under Will."
—Aleister Crowley, *The Book of the Law*

So wrote Aleister Crowley as being the creed of the pre-dominating energy that would influence every man and woman for the next 2,155 years. However, this comprehensive statement would be misunderstood and even attacked by his detractors.

The Will is the identifying purpose unique to each individual. It is the cause and purpose of the individual soul. It is the divine mold that is the real and omnipotent person. Being the "essence" of the soul, it has a very invincible power. Actually, the Will contains the source of one's power.

Will is the "place" each person has in the master plan. It is never the same for any two people (just as no two people ever have identical fingerprints). Yet collectively all Wills comprise a Greater Supreme Will. Each Will is like the prismatic colors that make up one light. The Great Work is the discovery of the true Will by removing the seekers' obstacles.

The Will exists before incarnation. A particular incarnation is chosen to complete past Karma. The Will is deeper than the intellect and the learned behavioral influences of parents, peers, media, etc. The illusory self or ego has been formed by influences such as society. Ignorance of the true Self propagates illusion. (Believing that manufactured knowledge is reality is called ego). For each person the lessons (obstacles) of such attainment are different. For example, some people rise above poor environment and others succumb to it. Some allow handicaps to restrict them and others become liberated as a result. The source of obstruction can be very sublime. What is constructive for one person may actually interfere with the Will of another, thereby becoming destructive (what is commonly called evil).

For example, a child has natural artistic tendencies from birth, but his father so influences him to become a lawyer that the child doesn't see his natural "calling." He goes on to be his father's creation, and may even be a fine, successful lawyer. He may also "learn" other qualities of life (standards of happiness) that are concurrently taught to him. However, in doing so he misses the experience of uniting with his own spirit.

Legend calls the misconception of one's Will, "the Fall." This is what separates man from God. Man is assigned to a higher (not perfect) state. Unity is this sweet taste of being one with God that man once knew that drives him to evolve back to that state.

> **"Every man and woman is a star."**
> —Aleister Crowley

Collectively each person in touch with his Will is the state of universal harmony with the Creator Itself! Once "perfected," each individual would be like a star traveling in its own orbit not intersection any other, functioning perfectly as a whole organism.

Who am I? Why did I choose to be born here? How does my past influence my present circumstance? What is my purpose? My true Self? My own individual role? My future?

The answer to these questions is never just handed out but must be reached through the karmic process of enlightenment.

To get in touch with your Will, you must start by identifying what is not your Will. As you strip away more and more of the intellectual illusion of the self and tame the ego, you will come closer to knowing your true purpose. The process is difficult and cannot be hurried.

> *Love is the Magickian's most important tool.*

Love is the Magickian's most important tool. Without it, he is impotent. Love is the execution of one's perfected Will, the force that unites form to spirit. Love can be called the substance of the universe. It is awesome to unite with the power behind every phenomenon and action. Thus the Magickian who unites with this omnipresent energy acquires certain powers which appear to the lay person as "miracles." This is certainly not the goal, but such powers come naturally as a result.

It is important not to confuse "love" as used here, with the ordinary social term. Although loving your neighbor is an aid to spiritual work (and society), the magickal meaning of love extends way beyond well beyond this concept. The word love itself has much import in gematria (numerical assignment) and in its correspondence to Chesed on The Tree of Life (see page 49).

Love occurs when each individual is doing his Will and every act he performs is a reflection of his true Will or purpose. These individual Will's have been created by God and are therefore part of God, the greater Will.

Knowing how to discover the true Will has been likened to the Philosophers Stone. It must be taught. There are no shortcuts. Those who desire to learn how to follow their true Will, become a perfect part of the drama of the universe and reach ultimate fulfillment.

The epitome of perfected man doing his Will; he is united with his higher self above the diversions of the elements.

The Purpose of Seeking Enlightenment

"Every man and every woman has a course, depending partly on the self, and partly on the environment which is natural and necessary for each. Anyone who is forced from his own course, either from not understanding himself, or through external opposition, comes into conflict with the order of the Universe, and suffers accordingly."

This passage from Aleister Crowley's *Magick in Theory and Practice* is crucial to the understanding and wisdom of this aeon. His name has been brought up several times in this book, not due to any special favoritism to him, but for the sole reason that his name is probably the most popular in the subject of Magick. People who have read his teachings as the "standard" of Magick can relate these two. Also, in studying the subject of Magick one will inevitably encounter his name and this book can hopefully place his often misunderstood Magickal teachings in proper perspective, as applied to our. Crowley was an occultist from the early 20th century surrounded by much controversy, but such judgment is irrelevant; what matters is the words rather than the person.

The purpose of pursuing a spiritual path is to seek and find the true self, which is the reflection of God, "perfection."

A path of enlightenment is only true if it can be of practical use for developing the soul and all its ramifications. A path which does not bring one to this state is not spiritual and may only be emotional.

Paths that require only devotion and obedience, or simple intuitive development alone, without teaching how to effect necessary changes in one's own life cannot enlighten; they can only teach philosophy. Most people follow such paths because they are the most common, and ubiquitous. They are popular because the only dedication they require is a simple agreement and intellectual comprehension of the basic precepts, and sometimes even a program to follow a given set of rules and customs.

Does the adherent of such paths obtain a usable benefit that is unique to that system? Or can one find the same benefit in less committed or narrow ways that are not classified as "divine"? A true course of enlightenment goes deeper than feel-good ideas.

Secondly, the goal of spirituality is to "evolve" to a higher state of uniting oneself with this God-force. Thus, when people become distracted by the goal aspect that a spiritual path offers, their purpose is no longer spiritual but a lust for reward. True spiritual results can only come when one is free of such desires.

The search for ones self entails understanding lower motivations and aspiring to the mystical mountaintop where all prophets have had their theurgic experiences. The entire process revolves around the light that nature casts upon the higher and lower self.

Also, one should not concern oneself with the progress of others. The aspirant must not forget that his work must be for his own development only. That is his obligation to himself, his fellow man, and his Creator.

When one is doing one's Will, it is not possible to have conflict with another. People are like plants. When each maintains his own orbit, all cooperate harmoniously, enjoying the solar family. If anyone were to fly out of its orbit, the system would fail and collapse into the sun.

Thus the gifts of attainment come to one who acts in unison with God; not just for the profane promises that some paths offer. If a person is unable to realize productive change and excellence in his daily life from his spiritual practices and devotion, why does he practice them?

While visible results should not be the only reason for pursuing spirituality, a valid spiritual path will provide them. Many spiritual paths depend on merely the psychological comforts they can provide to their constituents. One can use other vehicles for this purpose, a good talk with one's therapist or friend; attending an inspirational religious service; or chatting with one's hairdresser or the local bartender are a few of the alternatives that will serve this purpose! Spirituality should not exist just ot provide therapy, hope, or behavioral ethics.

Blind faith is not a good reason to follow a path either. A true spiritual teacher wants his aspirants to have divine experiences; thus the spiritual path is meant to enhance the aspirant's life. It is intended to allow the aspirant to learn what his individual Will is and how to fulfill it, thus revealing his life's purpose and karma. The Hermetic-Qabalistic path is one of many that provides knowledge of nature, the laws of the universe, called by some "God."

True spiritual attainment depends on no "Guru" and no method (Again let it be said that there is no one single key to The Great Work.) The"Guru" and path are only tools for the sincere. In this new aeon, each individual must find his own orbit. This does not mean that one can be self-taught, or that attainment will be handed to you by the Creator as if you were an Avatar—,[1] exempt from the restrictions of human beings!

The teacher is not your attainment! He is not your path. The true teacher is the vehicle that will guide your actions towards attainment. He is your link to "your higher-self," and he will teach you techniques that only you yourself can put into action. No teacher can implement these actions in your own soul.

---

1. Even Avatars have been taught. An Avatar is a direct formation of God into elements. These entities such as Christ, Buddha, Rosencreutz, Moses, Zarathustra, Amenhotep, etc. each had "missing" years in which they were schooled and consequently attained supernormally.

Though the multitude of "pop"-teachers will vehemently disagree, Baptism is your own doing and not the laying on of hands by any "superior!" You chose your incarnation. This New Age "let me give you the white light" and hackneyed "follow me because my *way* is centered around an Avatar whose works I've memorized in a four-year ashram program or similar seminar somewhere," don't work. History's most powerful magickal groups produced leaders, not hollow exhibitors of magickal forces found in many of today's more liberal magickal "clubs."

The teacher doesn't give you the "power"! He or she only brings you there—(If both are capable)! Only through working towards the mastery you've been taught including the hard and devastating failures, as well as those moments of success which can fool you into thinking that you've attained (if you're not careful), can your enlightenment be found.

So those who have been told that they can achieve what they want

> *Don't deny your Will by waiting for miracles to happen.*

by following a man or woman need to ask themselves "What have I been able to do? What have I seen? What have I experienced on a true mystical level?" The aspirant must only follow nature, not a mortal. Only by using nature are you able to open up to your higher self.

The true teacher does not put himself up on a pedestal for a follower of those who will feed his ego. A true master never announces his wisdom. He does not irrelevantly give a discourse on himself (a separate individual from you). It is the aspirant who succeeds or fails. The Guru, Method or Teacher is not responsible for your accomplishments or failures. There are times when either the gods or the devils will test you. Then the powers and endurance you learned from your teacher will be measured. Bear in mind the "partnership" responsibilities both must have of teaching and learning. And in those times when endurance fails, as it sometimes might, the magickal way is to go beyond endurance into the realm of Nature's power. This is the battle between light and darkness. Every tradition contains it, but only by repeated practice can the aspirant "invoke" it.

Don't deny your Will by waiting for miracles to happen. If you put forth the energy and still can't find the answer, that's okay. It will arrive when you are ready to receive it! Each person has only one Will, thus there is only one true path of enlightenment for him or her. God will discretely, at some time in life, present one with this path to "Godhood." It requires work to become a fit and worthy receptacle for enlightenment. If one were to encounter it before he was ready to receive it, he would not recognize it.

Likewise, if God were to indiscriminately let enlightenment come to everyone no matter what they did, the aspirant would be deprived of his quest. Man would already be perfect with no need to struggle through the obstacles that teach. If enlightenment was "meant to be" simply by being born, God would have already done it for you! Instead he gave only man a certain Will. Only a select few Avatars were given the secrets of perfection by God's divine intervention.

The search for ones self entails understanding lower motivations and aspiring to the mystical mountaintop where all prophets have had their theurgic experiences. The entire process revolves around the light that Nature casts upon the higher and lower self.

The New Aeon

We are on the brink of a new aeon.

Every 2155 years, the earth changes its "character." On the Vernal Equinox (March) of 1904 the Aeon (age) of Aquarius began.

The earth not only spins on its axis and orbits the sun, but the axis never stays perfectly erect. Gyroscopic action causes the axis to "wobble" slightly; that is the axis actually rotates in a very small circle. The earth completes this circle every 25,860 years. Therefore every 2155 years, the north pole of this axis moves clockwise 30 degrees (1 degree every 71.833333 years) which is equivalent to one zodiacal sign. The axis tilts, so does the equator, and the angle at which we observe the sun entering the belt of the Zodiac is the equinox. Every 2,155 years the earth comes under the influence of the next astrological sign. This is the prevailing energy that will influence the world for that period.

For example, from 251 B.C. to 1904 A.D., the earth's axis pointed toward Pisces, and all the properties of Pisces ruled:

—institutions and other large entities

—sacrifice

—religious establishments

—devotion

—prominence of enemy groups (i.e., secret enemies and armies)

In short, the Piscean aeon saw the organization of a powerful cult called Christianity. Also, we saw other great institutions form and enlist devotion from the governments of Rome to businesses like General Electric. Man emulated the sacrificial Christ as a model for himself.

Historians will find it interesting to take note of these 2155 year aeons and see how historical events correlate to them by astrological sign.

Preceding the Piscean aeon was the aeon of Aries (2406 BC up to 251 BC). At that time the planetary energy was Empirical; that is, great emperors ruled; all lands were conquered. Aries is assigned to the Emperor card. Like Aries, taking charge was imminent. Man wanted to dominate...either himself or other men. He learned to control his own life with the guidance of I-Ching; the concept of Tao was employed. Moses was then said to be the dominant "lawgiver" to the masses. Group oppression was giving way to group liberation. In Egypt, the Ram cult and the Ass cult proliferated, both being symbols of Aries.

A different god is "appointed" to rule each aeon. In the Egyptian system, the slain and sacrificed god, Osiris (later named Jesus Christ) ruled the aeon of Pisces. Khem ruled the aeon of Aries.

In this aeon we will see man grow from "adolescence" to "maturity"; he will "come into his own." Thus, the Egyptian god Horus, as the "crowned and conquering child," the god of completed man, is the ruler of this aeon.

> *The sign of Aquarius represents technology.*

If we compare an aeon to a day, we are literally minutes into this new, Aquarian aeon, 90 years! Now is an essential time for man to adjust to this change of "energy." The influence of Aquarius upon man is fruition, ingenuity, and culmination of purpose. Aquarius is the advancement of man as an individual. No more enmasse movements. Thus institutions, large corporations, governments, etc., are dissolving. Daily, smaller spiritual groups are forming, composed of individuals seeking enlightenment or ways to improve themselves. Never before in history has there been such a high rate of "new" or refounded spiritual groups as there is today! The idea of self sacrifice has transformed into self-improvement!

The sign of Aquarius represents technology. At the advent of this Aquarian age, within literally a minute into this aeon:
- —Man learned to fly!
- —Henry Ford invented the assembly line!
- —Einstein founded relativity!
- —Psychoanalysis was established!
- — Communications, radio, etc. spread!
- —Neils Bohr formulated the (well-known) model of the

atom, a center with orbiting electrons!
—New planets were discovered that would be signifi
   cant in man's "evolution"!
—Radium, bacteriology, etc., changed the practices of
   humanity!
—Man set foot on the moon!
—Profound computers were invented to dominate the hu
   man life and alter the entire course of the human race!

This 16th century illustration by Hans Weidetz depicts the master Mason teaching Magick (in this case, sacred construction) by experience instaed of by word. Learning Magick must be experienced, not just read about.

Every sign has its vices and virtues. In the last 50 years, man's bank of knowledge has doubled from what he has learned since his "birth." In the next ten years, this will double all signs of Aquarian energy. As you see, man can excel! He can also turn this energy of liberation against himself. The vice of Uranus (the ruler of Aquarius) is that its alluring offers can enslave. That is, something may seem so dazzling that it may be mistaken for ultimate perfection. Today's Uranian technology has been so abused that man surrenders his individuality to his own creations. Take the computer for example; many people are reliant on calculators, they can't do simple math anymore.

God, as individual Will, has been replaced by God as "whatever the computer says!" Man adapted a language for the computer, and then gave up his own language to speak "computerese." This has been the most regressive step in the history of mankind. Families spend more time around computers and television sets than developing personal growth experiences.

Man has assigned his native inner resourcefulness (aka spirit) to technology. Even as this is written, we must wade through the jungle of automated art to find a printed ad and people who are human beings!

> *For thousands of years, prophets have envisioned this time as the apex of mankind.*

Is Aquarian technology the tool of man to develop for his own wholistic perfection or is it a test to see if he is capable of seeing past these spiritless computers and recognize himself? The answer varies for each individual. For each individual has a Will that he must use, because this is the aeon of "individual Will." Those who become slaves of intellect and ego (the negative attributes of Aquarius) will be swept into the refuse by the natural flow of the Great Creation. Those who derive liberation out of "the gross matter" (as the alchemists put it so long ago) will change in harmony with nature (not challenge her). They will have nature's rewards realizing the positive attributes of Aquarius, the sign of "man."

For thousands of years, prophets have envisioned this time as the apex of mankind. This transition of aeons will not be easy, as we see. It is the judgment of each individual, *but* is judgment so devastating? No! It is the Gods and Goddesses providing mankind with the opportunity he needs to grow towards fulfillment.

Whatever path one takes, every individual will have to firmly decide what side of the fence to be on (i.e., to be in accordance with, or to be in opposition to nature). Is Magick the "fatalists' cure-all"? No, your fate is not predestined, you have the Will to shape it! Magick teaches how to cause any desired change. In this aeon, every individual must decide what approach to take toward the fulfillment of his own purpose. In the former Piscean aeon "fear of the Lord" was the only mentality required.

In this aeon there is no more "waiting for my ship to come in." You must go to it and then board it! Blind faith never works. Faith in what you have experienced (and therefore is not illusion or ego) does work.

Adepthood

An Adept is one who has endeavored and succeeded in living every moment of his or her life. "Inflamed" in spirit. This state can only be attained when one's consciousness is united with one's own Will. "Adept" is not simply a title bestowed upon one by a person in authority; it must be attained. It is a state of existence that is totally devoid of illusion.

"Once an Adept, always an Adept" is not the case. The Adept is not perfect and can fall if he is not wise. Before attaining to adepthood, one is taught the properties of this state and how to use and protect one's knowledge.

It is said that "no one sees what the Adept sees." Because the Adept has given up his ego, his actions often seem quite ordinary. Although one may perceive the presence of an Adept, it is a mistake to think that one understands him! If he is a true Adept, his actions are beyond an egotistical analysis. One should never try to see through the eyes of an Adept. To do so would cause an awful collision between illusion and folly where one becomes forever blinded by the flash of the impact. Keep in mind that the Adept is not God, but a representation of God. (Remember also, one must never follow just the teacher, but the path.)

It is of no purpose to know the spirituality or attainment of another. So to judge someone's spirituality or non-spirituality on any level always leads to failure. It is each person's duty to understand his own place in the universe as an individual with a unique Will.

What is the life of an Adept like? He or she chooses every activity according to his Will. He or she understands every act as a result of Adonoi ("God within and without"). He or she offers every action to God: eating, sleeping, breathing, teaching, learning, practicing, working, playing, etc. Many of his or her daily activities may be the same as those of the non-adept, but the Adept realizes that every act is a manifestation of his Will. Actions, thoughts, feelings, come directly from the higher self of which he or she is always cognizant. None of the adept's actions are circumstantial, although he or she can make them so to teach or for other reasons. In short, the Adept makes every act a ritual and receives the same profound elation from these mundane acts as he or she would from the most supreme rituals of evocation! Keep in mind however, an Adept doesn't do this for the purpose of devotion. Although devotion is essential, any ordinary religious man may be truly devoted to the laws of his religion without ever even reaching the first steps of adepthood.

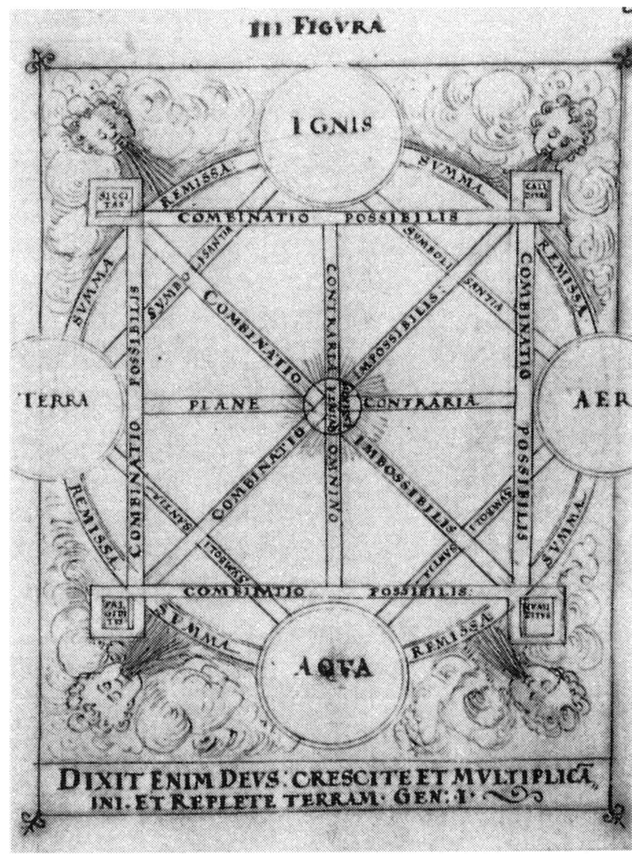

The Sylva Philosophorum, from the 1600's was lais out by Cornlelius Petraeus. It is a formul;a which helps to explain certain Magickal phenomenon. Like all such knowledge, it can not explain the source of that phenomenon, nor does it presume to try to do so.

What does adepthood feel like? Because adepthood is total infusion with spirit, there is no way to describe this state in words. The Adept has given up anything that for even the briefest moment will separate him or her from this state; Adepts remain an Adept under any conditions, so nothing can move them. Thus the derivation of the word "adapt" from Adept.

According to several Hermetic Orders, one is technically an adeptus minor when one has attained to Tiphareth on the Tree of Life.

Faith

Magick is not the illusion of hoping that one can merely have some emotional or intellectual experience. Of what value is a system that is limited to just ordinary experience? Theory is not the practice of spirituality. Truths can be seen. The Magickal tradition neither depends on nor requires blind faith.

One of the finest things of Hierophancy is the knowledge one receives from his students. As we sat one day and discussed this subject, a student told me a story that was part of his family's religious tradition. Perhaps you have heard it, but I shall recount it here for you anyway:

A flood overcame a man's house. A first boat came by to save him. He said, "I believe God will save me." The water rose. He went upstairs. A second boat offered him a means to leave. Again his ego/intellect believed God would save him. Finally, as the man climbed to his roof, a helicopter gave him his last chance. The man still waited for God. The man drowned.

Upon "meeting his maker," he said, "God! I had faith, but didn't even see you! What happened? Why?"

God said, "What's the matter? You didn't see the two boats and the helicopter I sent for you?"

God will provide an act that you will receive (or divine) for the purpose of informing you of Its existence. It then soon withdraws behind the veil of Isis forever until you have arduously climbed through the obstacles of a lifetime to Its throne.

Often eager believers claim to have "seen" divinity, when they've seen nothing, but only thought it. How many times have people professed to have heard deity's words when of course, they really didn't. These people are the blind faith believers and the dead.

To believe that just because you are Its creation It will converse with you, is arrogant. If this were so, you would be above the angels and they below you. Godhood requires perfection and Its displays are discreet. They are not pearls before swine.

He or she who has been privileged by a true "unexplainable" manifestation should not expect the Gods to perform for them on call. To be worthy of utilizing the highest force, one must be of truth and beyond illusion. The magickal precept is that one should only believe what they have experienced, with no wishful delusions. The force of God is there for those who have been schooled in the divine methods of communication. Such persons (i.e., the Magickian, sage, magi, etc.) may attract Its manifestation at Will.

Faith occurs upon receiving a true divine substantiation. And even then, the profane may interpret anything convenient for their needs to relieve them of human misery—or escape. There is no escape. Thus the Magickian harnesses and conquers his circumstance to rise above these human weaknesses. God never intended for man to be weak. That is why It made man the dominant species of the planet.

It is said by the ancients, "Woe to he who has been chosen to have divine experience of 'occult' manifestation and does not use the path along which God made this gift occur!" For he can know no other way to know God (except intellectual perception which is valueless), but for the one and only place God has chosen to show Its action before him. For once in Its "garden" one cannot go to other places where God is to seek It. God chooses a time and place for such experiences and is not at the whim of the aspirant to expect this relationship to be altered. Such a link cannot be broken by any law of science other than going against the laws of nature which is blasphemous. Remember, God does not concede to any of his creation. God's laws are made for man to live in accordance with.

> *The seeker must perform and seek truth—not just intellectual knowledge.*

Any power harnessed and produced in this material world is like a battery (having two opposite poles). The religious promotion that God, or Its manifestations express only one half (the benign half) of a totality is a device of the promotional department of the church, ashram, etc., or it may be their ignorance for they themselves may be aspiring devotees. God will not alter the Laws of the Universe that he created because you desire! Those energies know no mores, just actions of a similar harmonious nature like a radio transmitter and receiver. It is God's wrath that destroyed the destroyers. It is God's teaching method called karma that may perhaps inflect pain or sorrow.

The modern and easy excuse of "if it is meant to be" etc., is very old. Many deprived people sit without food believing if God meant for their families to eat, God would provide! In arabic, this concept is the term *inshallah*.

The seeker must perform and seek truth—not just intellectual knowledge. Knowledge is abundant. Attainment is the acceptance of secrets within as brought out by the spiritual teacher.

Faith is required based on the student who has known of true magickal experiences which have preceded previously. But the greatest faith is that of the teacher in the aspirant, and not vice versa as some would believe. How arrogantly some so-called students approach their spiritual teachers.

The Ego and Intellect

In order to attain in the Hermetic system, the ego and the intellect must be controlled, because they restrict one from contacting the higher self. It is this true self that is able to see and perform things of a more sublime nature.

Realize that both the universe and man defy rational explanation. You or any other person can not analyze the universe—in the microcosm or the macrocosm. It is above intellectual perception but not above our sensitive intuitive perception. It can only be described by multidimensional experience individually.

No one can explain why the laws of science exist. Yet science attempts to intellectualize how the universe was formed and why! Scientists's theories get more absurd every year.

Although science is sure it can "prove" (i.e., intellectualize or rationalize) man evolved from other animals, they cannot find the missing link to definitely prove it. Where did it go? Everything else seems to fit so neatly.

They can always explain the phenomenon of how certain elements came together to form life, they cannot reproduce the process although the physical combination is easy to analyze. It is only just recently that scientists have recognized the missing element of Spirit! So, these and other "mysteries" cannot be rationalized.

Freud calls the act of creating an answer on principal, when some of the data is missing, "projection."

The willingness to overcome obstacles in order to make spiritual progress is necessary for sincere aspirants.[1] They must let go of attachments that harbor fear of the unknown, or self-created answers for that which is unknown particularly within themselves. Such "answers" are obstacles because they are mistaken for knowledge and reality, instead of recognized for what they truly are: ego/illusion; igno-

---

1. The laws of nature will work for you if you work with them. Look at the fulcrum, a lever based on the law of gravity. Depress this lever, and it can lift tons. This is an act of Magick.

rance of the true self. Letting go of such attachments are not really sacrifices at all! They liberate the trapped soul who settles for existence instead of life. Humans are conditioned to modify their Will to: a) the standards of others; b) the standards of organizations; c) their current way of life; d) an acceptable illusion of what is considered to be fulfilling; e) restrictions they believe and accept.

> *The role of the spiritual teacher is to strip away the shell of arrogance from the aspirant so that he can experience another level of perception ...*

Ego/Illusion is the enemy of the Magickian. Though this may sound purely philosophical, it is purely practical, because making a mistake on this path can be fatal or at least injurious. The aspirant's inability to distinguish reality from illusion is like the Devil card in the Tarot, which has a large open eye in order to see, because it can only see the physical appearances. The practice of any system of enlightenment requires the aspirant to learn to tap into the divine energy, rather than just the physical.

Often the mistake is made of confusing human emotional experience for divine ultra-human experience, although each has its proper place. The belief that the student can determine this without guidance is termed arrogance. Thus, in a true learning process, the aspirant is taught to think for himself, and must choose to either: a) learn to understand his own thoughts and emotions, or b) believe that he has the perception to distinguish reality, without being affected by his prejudices, likes or dislikes, fears, etc.

The aspirant is always given the chance, within certain limitations, to experiment; to find out if what he "knows" is true or false. With guidance, the aspirant learns to distinguish. One is ready to learn when one puts aside all preconceived notions of what reality is. This requires unconditional humility on the part of the aspirant.

The role of the spiritual teacher is to strip away the shell of arrogance from the aspirant so that he can experience another level of perception, where he will encounter things alien to his mode of thinking. Most people are taught to think; the Magickian is taught not to think. The universe, as well as the miracle of man himself, is neither rationale nor thinkable-these things are incomprehensible to the limited intellect. Thus, the teacher brings the aspirant to a level beyond words and self-centeredness.

Once the aspirant has mastered one set of forces (verified by his teacher) he will need to make further sacrifices. (Sacrifice is divesting oneself of that which restricts his own Will and is not really a sacrifice as you know it.) Sacrifice which restricts the Will rather than acting to free it is, of course, destructive. This type is epidemic among almost all society.It is a disease. The divine sacrifices can only be dispensed by one's teacher who knows what is constructive and destructive to the student. Generally, no two aspirants have the same things to sacrifice. The most ingrained habits (even those that actually seem ot be beneficial) when sacrificed give control back to the individual. To the Magickian, all acts must be by choice and willful intent.

Sacrificing a vice is sometimes not what the student desires to do. It is the resistance to the Will, and threat to the ego that causes one to rationalize his dark side.[2] But having faith that these disciplines are for the aspirant's own good inspires him to work even harder for more control over circumstances so he can reach that ultimate mastery of Will, unity, and perfection—a very blissful and ecstatic state!

Even in the most difficult spiritual exercises and tests, the aspirant must be receptive to new experiences, for when the teacher has taught him fully, he will be able to see and know all for himself. Then he is ready to obtain magickal gifts.

---

2. Each person has both a light and dark side until perfection is reached.

The Power of the Mind

The "powers of the mind" come from deep within the individual, not from the intellect. The study which delves into such obscure regions can be generally labeled occult.

Within each man and woman is a universal force able to cause change both subjectively and objectively. The fervent beat of the drum that slowly evokes one's emotional energy upward and outward has been effectively practiced for years, by tribes around the globe. Various cultures have mastered raising the group-energy and directing it at certain individuals or causes by focusing their mind on dolls or photos. Today some high-energy concerts, "holy-roller" church groups, advertisements and even movies have used (and abused) these methods to possess the group energy for their own personal interests. How often have you heard of football games that have incited riots? The impact of such emotional outbursts affirm and strengthens one's relationship to the love object or ideal.

Recorded accident reports of the 115-pound woman who lifts the front end of her car off her child's chest document the superpower of the mind. Although the woman states that "she doesn't know" how she did it, she always agrees that muscular strength was not the force (see diagram opposite page).

Mind control is the essential basis for all systems of enlightenment because it is impossible to control any forces of Nature without being able to control those complimentary forces within the self. Any energy that you invoke takes on your personal influence as it passes through you into manifestation.

The purpose of developing mental powers (only a tool which leads to control of emotional and spiritual insights) is to make yourself a fit receptacle for force *that you will*, so as to lead you to the perfection you see. It is not intended to be used for controlling the Will of others!

A Note on Channelling:
Many people claim to receive "channeled messages" from

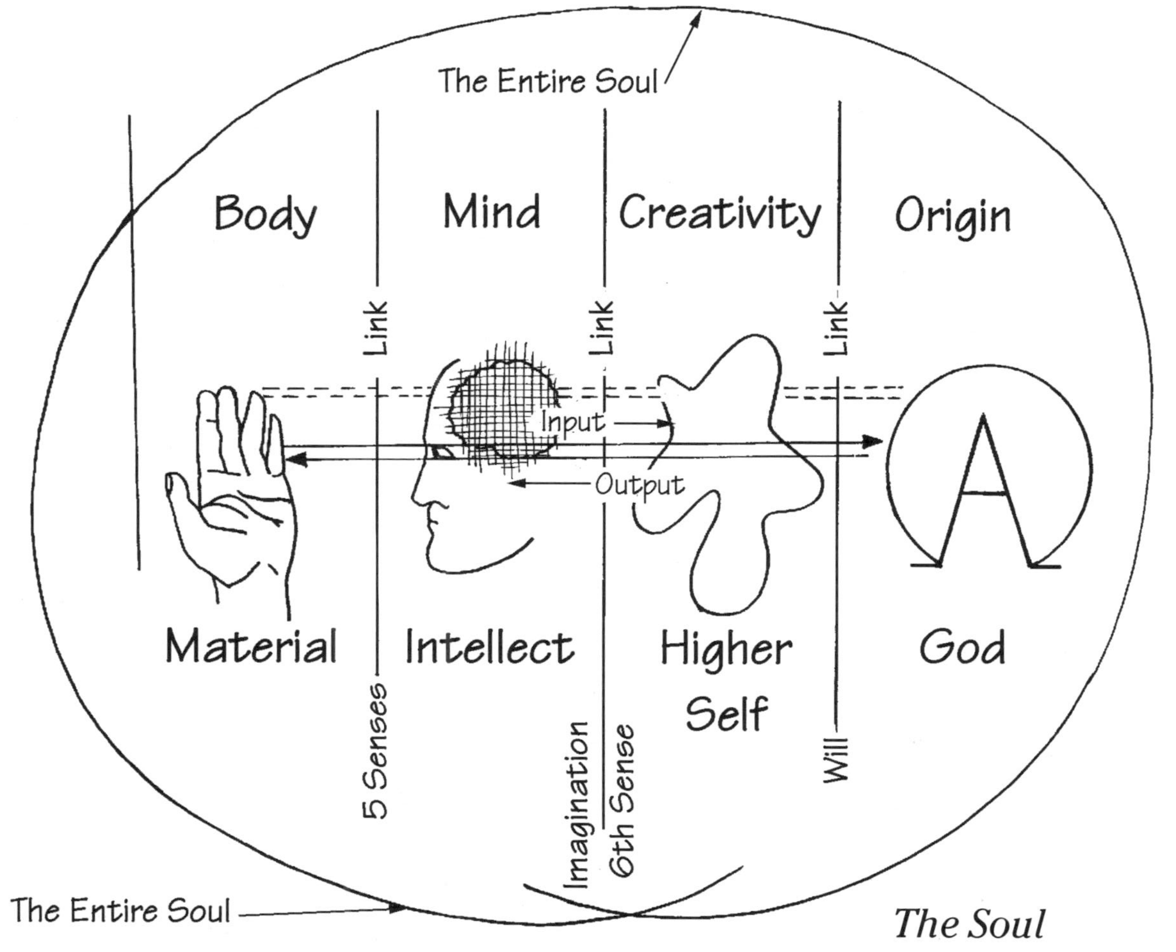
The Entire Soul
Body
Mind
Creativity
Origin
Link
Link
Link
Input
Output
Material
Intellect
Higher Self
God
5 Senses
Imagination
6th Sense
Will
The Entire Soul
The Soul

exalted beings; most of them openly confess they never had any experience with the occult! In keeping with eternal magickal tradition, only attained masters and avatars can be handed wisdom. Christ Himself had to dedicate several hidden years to study Magick (despite the movie *Last Temptation of Christ*, that shows him as an ordinary man who one day had a seizure and woke up enlightened).

Why would these exalted masters or enlightened beings from other planets share their wisdom with those who are still working out their karma, Saturn-returns and other problems?

We cannot rule out the possibility that such communications might occur. Such narrow-mindedness can deny one spectacular results and judgment is not a mortal ability. But how many Cleopatras, Pharoahs, King Arthurs, Atlanteans, or other reincarnated greats are there running around today? A rash of people who believed they were the reincarnation of Billie Holiday occurred when the movie *Lady Sings The Blues* was around. There was a time when Napoleanism was popular, and all the reincarnated Napoleons emerged. Are the Elvises next?

This is not to make fun, but only to draw attention to a much more prevalent phenomena today: The "self-enlightened" Magickian. Thanks to the New Age, "spirit guides" have become popular, translating into an old concept of ascended masters for the deeper occult enthusiasts. These "chosen ones" (of which there are an enormous number) hear voices, or rationalize philosophical deductions given to them as enlightenment.

Although each person is capable of exceptional things, and linked within each soul is divine wisdom, miracles are far and few between. Yet divine intervention can manifest itself to an enthusiast who does not go around espousing his spirituality. Usually one must arduously prepare and properly invoke for such revelatory experience. Even then, intellect can disguise itself as authentic! (Look at the great occultists. None have ever claimed spontaneous Mastership). Nature does not give a tree the right to grow, flourish, and reproduce without water, soil and sunlight.

The Subconscious

So, here is how the magikal processes of the mind actually *do* work:

Often the subconscious makes a cameo appearance to the cognitive mind. The subconscious is so foreign that it can be mistaken as a separate entity—apart from its neighboring conscious. Thus many "channellers" are only channelling their own subconscious impressions.

Magickal praxis integrates both parts of the self, as seen in the formula of the Hexogram (see pg. 2). Awareness rises above intellect, by breaking down the barrier to the subconscious, allowing the next step of integrating the total mind (conscious and subconscious) with the individual soul.

In Qabalistic terms: *first*, recognition of the body occurs (the Assiah) *then* identity (intellect) called "mind" develops (the Yetzirah). In Magick one delves into hidden secrets of the "other" self, the subconscious (called Briah). Subconscious is not only influenced from the intellect (Yetzirah) and outside stimulus, but the hidden side or spirit (called Atziluth) and divine stimulus.

Man's body is born in Malkuth, the elements. His higher-self, which is above mortal influences, exists in Tiphareth or the Christ-self. But in looking up at Tiphareth from Malkuth, one sees an obstacle—Yesod, the subconscious. So one is taught to clear out and open the subconscious so it may act as a lens to Tiphareth (and thereby contact the higher self). Remember, further, that Tiphareth is directly under the influence of Kether (perfection, unity, God).

If the aspirant is not aware of his or her own inner mind (buried subconscious), any information it receives from the intellect can seem to be outside itself—as coming from another "being" or source! This "being" may be assigned a separate identity. Its "revelations" can really be the contents of the subconscious and should not be mistaken for information dispensed by a separate third party entity. Such material is purely subjective. It is every single impression from the past (even past lives) of that individual.

The subconscious does not have the ability to forget (it only represses things in its subconscious bank). One's impressions, traumas, etc., always have the urge to come out. They express themselves in the language of the subconscious. When such subconscious material (unique to that individual) emerges, it may be interpreted as divine communication instead of just a part of the person they never knew was inside of them.

With proper guidance, subconscious appearances can be dealt with and resolved. Ignoring the subconscious denies the aspirant the discovery of his self and what occurs within. If dispensed to others, this information becomes a mere projection of the aspirant's personality eccentricities. It is then represented as "higher knowledge," and others may actually follow the expression of the channeller's Will, without knowing it!

It is imperative then, that as one undertakes occult work, he or she masters and utilizes the subconscious to its maximum. Then higher information which is truly valid and emanating from Atziluth/spirit (sometimes called angels, etc.) will be unaffected by its passage through the operator's mind.

When people advertise their divine informants, question it. When you think you are privy to divine knowledge, interpret it subjectively; it may have an important relationship to your true personality and growth.

Who is God?

In Magick, God is not comprehensible to the limited mind of man. "It" is the one impermeable, undefinable, unlimited "thing yet no thing," above all form. It is not even confined to man's definition of force. Force and form are only physical manifestations of God. A simple and similar analogy is to compare hydrogen and oxygen. They are both distinct. When combined, a third new homogenous substance is formed that is not hydrogen or oxygen. It is called water. God is the phenomenon of nature (meaning the "natural course of events," not simply trees and butterflies.) God is Nature.

God does not conform to the customs of man. "It" is above such restrictions as male or female, force or form. Both are "born" from "It." Thus both are complementary halves of a whole which is a third "state."[1] God is not intellectual. "It" does not judge to meet the standards of a theology. "It" is not prejudiced.

> *God does not conform to the customs of man.*

God, gravity, matter, personality, air, life, time, law, chaos, etc. are "laws/principles" that are beyond human understanding.

However, to attempt to intellectualize God, man has created God in his own image, from culture to culture. This formulation is then assigned in ethical system, an organization called "religion." Man gave God human eyes and a brain! To the aborigines God is one thing, to the early Romans, It was another, to the Jews yet another, and it goes on and on!

A scholarly look at the biblical phrase "God made man in his own image" is often used by those who don't know the difference between "image" and "imagination" and can't recognize creation without scientific explanation. They as-

---

1. See the supernatural triangle on the Tree of Life, page 57.

sume the identification of "HIS." (As if God has a gender and looks a certain way.)

Who originally translated "image"? If a thing is made in image (in this case man), it is not yet manifest and is superior to the confinement of elements. An "image," according to the qabalistic four-world system, is not on the same plane as physical manifestation.

More importantly, our culture's arrogant psychoanalysis of God's actions (e.g. grace and condemnation) is merely what man interprets to conform to his own behavior.

The laws of nature demonstrate that all corporeal bodies must come to an end! If man was immortal it would be unnatural, because nothing physical lasts forever. To believe in human immortality is against the laws of nature.

So if God is eternal and does not exist on the physical plane, where does that leave the theist? With a concept different from his own framework!

Thus, an immortal phenomenon such as "God," is incomprehensible to man's three-dimensional, physical brain. The phenomena of nature demonstrate that intellect is insufficient for a true level of understanding. Higher Magickal experience replaces man's intellect. This transcendence is also beyond man's identifiable feelings. It leaves a more subtle path which is deep in each person, called the "arcane," the "secret," "occult," or the "unknown." Didn't the ancient wise men say "one cannot see the face of God and live?" They meant one had to transcend the confines of human experience to understand and unite with this true God!

Since It is unmanifest, there exists "no face of God"! Thus the paradox:

1) All manifestation lives.

2) Life, (not man) it is said, is immortal, for "Life energy is beyond the chemical constituents of the finite body" (the elements).

The alchemical insinuation that there is no waste in nature indicates that all is one. Though things are separated by imperfection and incompleteness, when all things recombine with the creative force, the physical plane will not exist. Man will live as one with his soul. The state of perfection unites the chemicals of one body or thing to its other "body" without diminution, or ego-separation. This is the ancient way of attempting to describe steps to individual attainment. It carries through into every religion and philosophy, though its symbols and interpretations may vary from path to path.

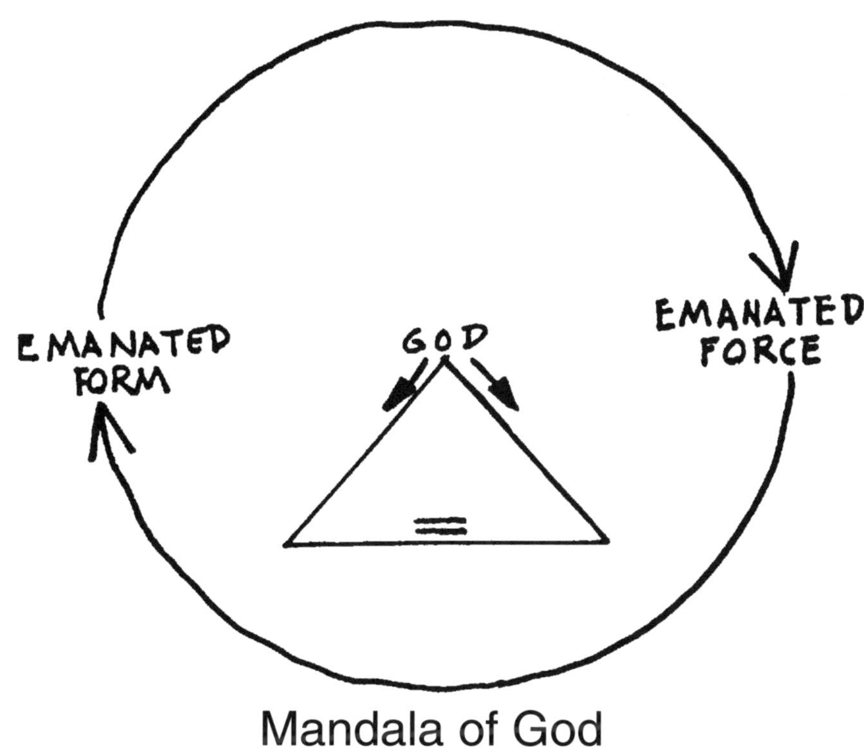

Mandala of God

So "God" is soul, eternal and personal. It is perfection in creation and reflected in the perfected part of the human being. Thus, to speak of one's perfected self is to claim to be able to "identify" a transcended, multidimensional soul. It is an egotistical thought, a rationale that reduces this indescribable, universal and awesome phenomenon to common words. Speaking about one's relationship with God inhibits the perfected God-self from liberation from its more base ego-formed attachments that dominate. Such espousement reinforces illusion. One's sacred identity, if reduced to mere coffee-table chatter, gets wrapped up by the shroud[2] of base limitations.

2. The shroud of Turin was Mary Magdelane's act of covering up Christ's identity. She wanted to hide him using ego.

In the Egyptian tradition, the Goddess Isis wanted to be united with the soul of the high god Ra. However, being an individual she wasn't perfect, just an aspect of the whole of creation, and limited to only bear life and not form. Thus if the name of God is not pronounced, but if one unites with it as a symbol, the manifestation of that individual ego would be annihilated and one's own personal perfection would ensue.

How can man refer, then, to God? Him? Her?, It?, etc. God is All and (above "allness") no *thing*! Wisdom, not words!

The multitudes of people who follow the ideas of Man are lead into the depths of pain and illusion.

Who is Satan?

Satan is the god[1] that people hate. Man builds his own Satan. It keeps the ignorant bound to each other. Further, anything that threatens that bond (out of ignorance) is labeled evil.

People fear and even hate liberation and truth when it threatens their egos. For the ignorant, it is easier to shriek and condemn truth rather than to confront those inevitable forces that will expose their own "devilishness." It is actually harder to acknowledge one's "darker self" than it is to conquer and transform it. Ego creates this avoidance technique yet few realize that each person is born imperfect!

The person who teaches the acknowledgment of truth and liberation may become the object of hate by the ignorant. Any object, idea, person, etc., that people hate is decried and judged not good; evil; clinically, it becomes a Satan.

> *Man builds his own Satan.*

The perpetrator of fraud is always right or so he believes. He rationalizes all his actions calling them "good" or "God's work." He defames anyone or anything that is not understood by the exact definitions of his program. And since he does not consider the possibility that he could be wrong, he must be "good" and others "evil."

This rationale has gotten the world into grave trouble. Hitler feared those who might be threatening "his" race, so he murdered them! So did the Christians, who killed the growing threat of "paganism," in order to "eliminate the competition." Even the Christians themselves were thrown to the lions to demonstrate the Roman Empire's "superiority."

When a person devotes his life-energy in pursuit of a desired

---

1. God is a generic term encompassing all divine energies. That energy does not have to be particularly adoring. Energy devoted to any end is all that is required. The energy which is evil and destructive is the God called Satan.

goal, then IT is their God. When they become so obsessed with an end result that it usurps and possesses them, it is "anti-god," i.e., their Satan.

For example, when your lover admires another's attributes, you may demean that person by defaming those attributes. Thus your alleged "goodness" oppresses that person's "no-goodness." You become "right," that other person thus becomes "bad", "wrong" i.e. "Satan" (although called other more socially accepted names). So, Satan is created by man!

Levi's depiction of Baphomet represents the restrictive forces of nature.

In reality, one can unite with or defy God by one's relationship to the mechanics of the universe. Satan is the force which separates man from God. Truth (freedom from illusion) can eliminate this separative force. According to ancient texts, this aeon will be born within each individual. The "Messiah" of this aeon will not be any exterior circumstance or event. The resulting collective group-consciousness will be based on perfecting the self.

In order for liberation[2] to occur, the attachments and weaknesses of the lower part of the self must be overcome. The truth[3] is divine. When a person overcomes this restrictive force, that true understanding brings him or her closer to wisdom. Rebellion of the ego to maintain its hold will appear. But he or she who seeks liberation from the unnatural curses of mortal obstacles is taught to understand and control the falseness of ego.

2. Liberation is extrication from that which restrict one's Will. Such restrictions are a) self imposed or b) circumstances that the individual allows to possess or restrict him.
3. Truth is not a moral concept, but an actual perception of reality free from deception.

Individuality is fundamental to this new age. Liberation is its theme. There can be no more group following, which served the old aeon, when slavery became rampant. Separately, all people will seek enlightenment until this unit of individual perfection of the human race is complete. This is why so many new spiritual groups are emerging today.

The ego is not destroyed in this process but becomes subordinate to the higher self. The taming of the ego can only be taught by those enlightened ones who have already learned to reconcile and master it! They must be free of the "hang-ups" that their students are trying to conquer. The proper teacher will appear to those who are ready. Man cannot educate himself.

PART TWO

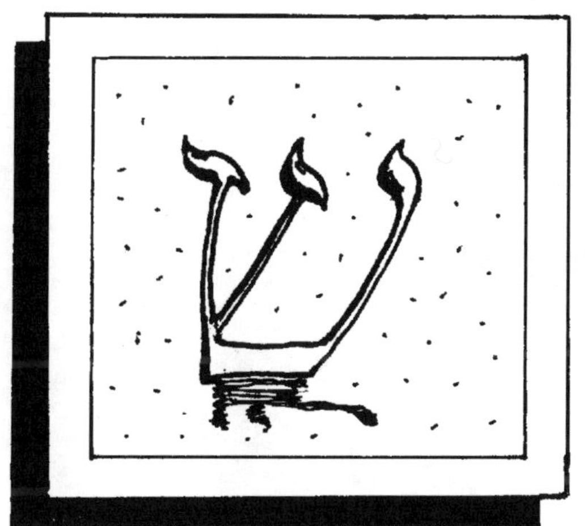

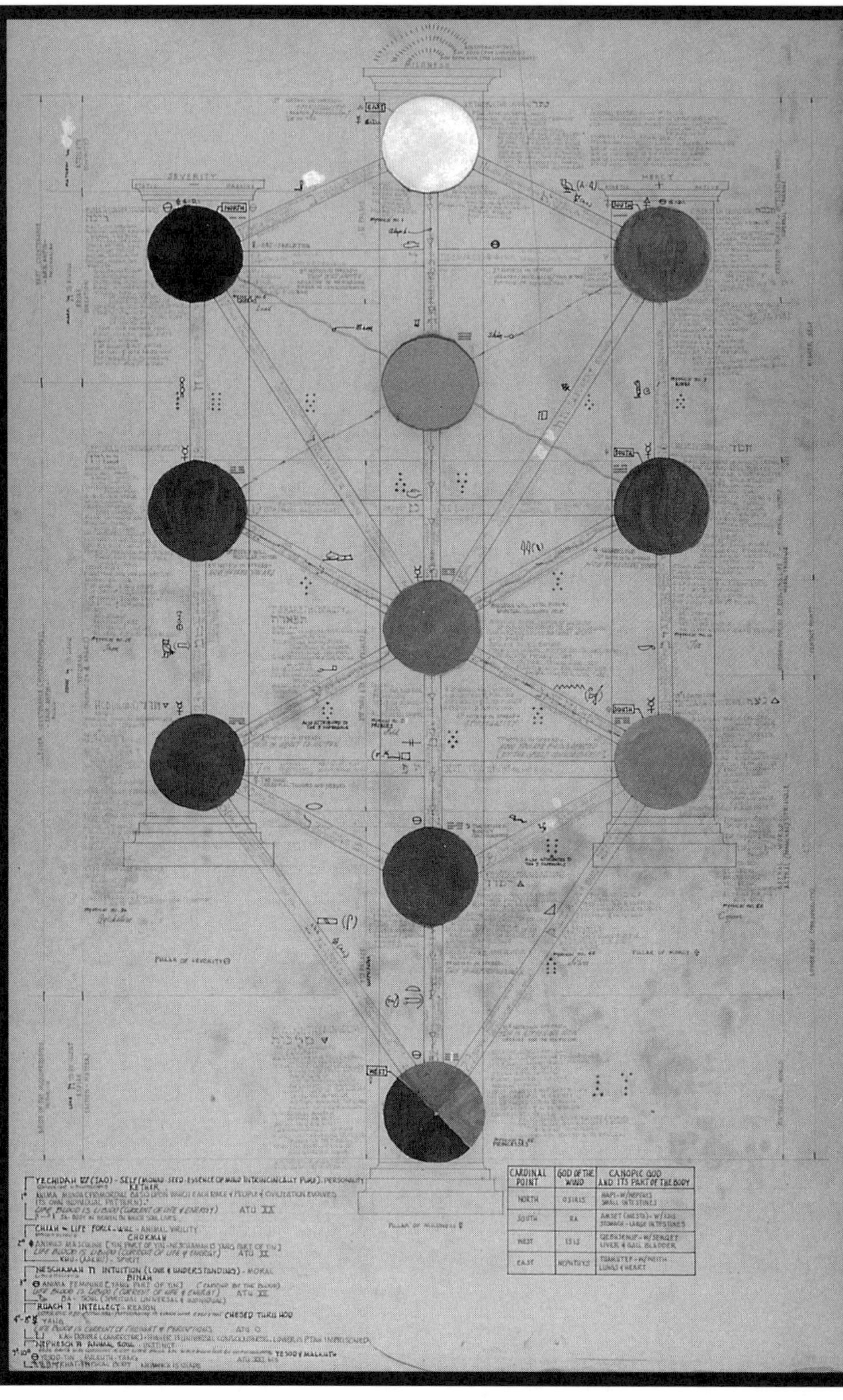

CARDINAL POINT	GOD OF THE WIND	CANOPIC GOD AND ITS PART OF THE BODY
NORTH	OSIRIS	HAPI - W/NEPHYS, SMALL INTESTINES
SOUTH	RA	AMSET (MESTA) - W/ISIS, STOMACH - LARGE INTESTINES
WEST	ISIS	QEBSENUF - W/SERQET, LIVER & GALL BLADDER
EAST	NEPHTHYS	TUAMUTEF - W/NEITH, LUNGS & HEART

Facing page. Early "Tree of Life" plate by the author.

"The Specifics"

What Is Qabalah?

Here is a simple explanation of the Qabalah that readers familiar or unfamiliar with it will be able to understand. Qabalah is, however, a verbal tradition and can only be fully understood through formal teaching.

Just as the symbol of a musical note can be understood and played only by someone taught to read it on a musical chart, so too does the Qabalah consist of symbols that represent the unseen forces that are part of life.

Every spiritual philosophy uses a system based on the Qabalah, which is the study of the Tree of Life, because every phenomenon in the universe corresponds to one of the energies on the Tree. Its purpose is to help us understand, categorize, relate to, and utilize certain abstract forces (wisdom) of anything. And this process itself allows the individual to absorb any wisdom just by the use of Qabalah. By assigning them symbols, we make these abstract ideas assimilable, as you'll see.

There are ten expressions of spirit in manifestation ("forces") which are called sephiroth (sephirah, singular). Connecting these are 22 paths. These form a glyph which is the Tree of Life (see page 49).

Kether:

Out of so-called "nothingness" (which actually has a value but is not manifested), emanates the first state of existence which is the primal source (creator) of all the other sephiroth. Kether is therefore the source of everything, it is total and absolute unity of all with no restrictions. Kether has no limitations of form or force. Everything is a part of and has emanated from Kether. It is the essence of purity; for by its totality it lacks nothing and is thus perfection. Thus we can attribute God to Kether. White, like a light, it is made up of several other colors.

Chokmah:

A fragment of the primal energy Kether characterizes itself in the second sephirah, Chokmah. Chokmah expresses Kether as any defined identity. As number two, it is the state of duality and polarity. It is a defined reflection of any specific aspect of Kether. Chokmah means wisdom in English. Chokmah is Kether's separation into opposites and thus a particular force manifests that is yang, male, and outgoing (i.e. active). Chokmah is unique and true identification as originally issued from the "conglomerate-identity" of Kether. Thus, the white of Kether becomes gray in Chokmah by being separated from the primal source.

At right. The sephiroth are the circles emanating from the top down. the paths connect them are syntheses of them. Sephiroth and paths are numbered. The Ain is the state of negativity; Ain Soph is anything that is limitless; Ain Soph Aur is the light which is limitless. These are unseen forms of existence and the Tree evolves out of it. The Qliphoth are the forces called evil demons. These forces have no soul and can't attain on the Tree.

AIN SOPH AUR
AIN SOPH
AIN
1 KETHER
3 BINAH
2 CHOKMAH
5 GEBURAH
4 CHESED
6 TIPHARETH
8 HOD
7 NETZACH
9 YESOD
10 MALKUTH
DAATH
MAGUS 2.
FOOL 1.
EMPERESS 4.
PRIESTESS 13.
HIEROPHANT 6.
CHARIOT 8
LOVERS 7.
LUST 19.
EMPEROR 5.
HERMIT 10.
ADJUSTMENT 12.
FORTUNE 11.
HANGEDMAN 15.
DEATH 14.
DEVIL 16.
TOWER 17.
SUN 20.
STAR 18.
AEON 21.
UNIVERSE 22.
MOON 19.
SEVERITY
MERCY
MILDNESS

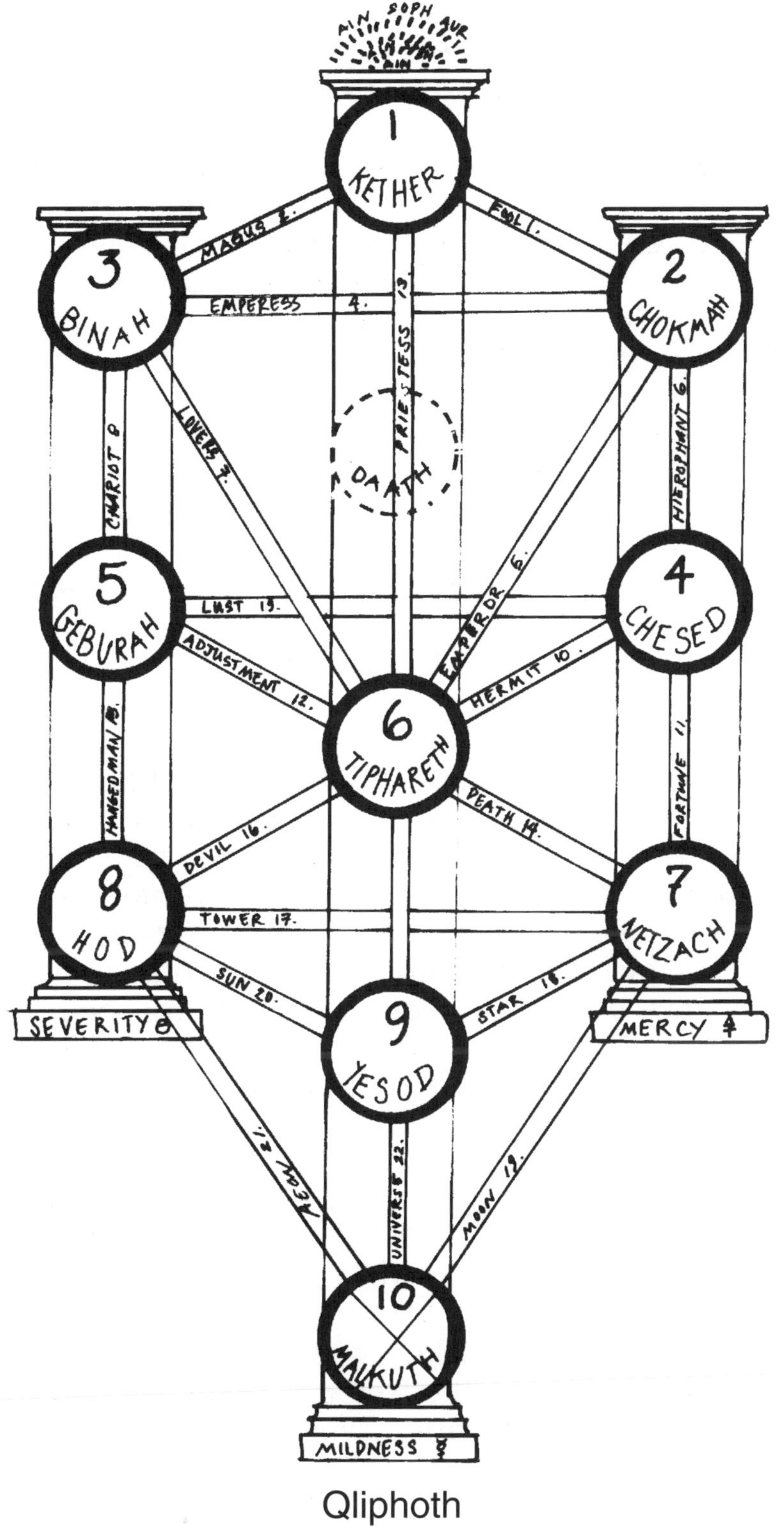

Qliphoth

Binah:

Since the Qabalistic Tree is constructed on balance and compliments in existence, this third emanation manifests in the sephirah called Binah which is the form that the identity of Chokmah takes, i.e., expression of this primary Chokmah energy. Think of Binah as the divine medium that carries the divine character (Chokmah). It is the third integral expression of Kether, the state of perfection (being the Polar opposite of wisdom and being under the direction dissemination/flow of the "fountain which flows from Kether"). It is literally understanding.

One cannot have understanding without wisdom, and one cannot be wise unless one truly understands (not merely knows). Chokmah and Binah are complimentary expressions of perfection.[1]

The most fundamental aspect of Binah is that it is the true unaltered receptacle, yin and female. Because it is black it receives all of the primal light from Kether.

Daath:

From Binah this same energy which originated in Kether progresses downward along the Tree across the invisible sephirah called Daath, which is absolute and true knowledge. Here (like the asteroid belt which was a former planet) is a sephirah that doesn't really "exist." As manifestation, it is the "True Will" which provides knowledge not only of "external" circumstances, but more importantly, of the True Self.

One knows nothing about what one perceives if relying only on appearance, assumption, or learned intellect. Daath is where descriptive words leave off and the experience of both wisdom (Chokmah) and understanding (Binah) begin. By looking at the Tree (see diagram page 49) you see Daath is the "resultant" of the Supernals. Here, man experiences the forces of the very Creation itself as well as the forces of the "Fall" of man in reality!

Daath is absolute truth, where no falsehood or illusion exists. However, in the ascent up the Tree, the Adept faces his greatest challenge in crossing the abyss where Daath lies, and which

---

1. "To know is one thing; to understand...that is the point."
          —Albert Einstein

separates Godhood from mankind's cognitions and lesser tools. Binah is the first step above human perception toward God perfection. Daath is between.

In Daath both the Devil and God are represented as follows: Human perception is an illusion of what truly exists. Superhuman perception is reality with no human obscurities. This cohabitation of these two conflicting forces is neither one nor the other. In ascending up the Tree one resides in Chesed or moves on to Binah with no stopover in this invisible Daath.

The abyss contains all the illusions, deceptions, traits, and restrictions of mankind as well as alien and profound dimensions of the Creator. The Creator knows no restrictions of up and down for both are one. This also applies to all man's concepts: black/white, solid/liquid, manifest/non-manifest, past/future, etc.

Crossing the abyss transforms the soul from the lessons of mortal laws to nonhuman, Godlike, universal phenomena.

Chesed & Geburah

Becoming yet more dense and manifest, this energy next transforms into Chesed, the 4th sephiroth the state of manifestation known as mercy. A calm lake with an occasional ripple is an example of Chesed's energy. Chesed is how man translates the first three sephiroth into a comprehensible form; the first expression of divine origin to human comprehension. It is higher love, e.g., man's capability of uniting to all existence. This leads to Godhood, as mentioned above. "Love is the law" means uniting to (and ending separation from) all that exists ("combining with" in compassion), both "lovers," though not loosing their individual Wills.

Opposite to this passive expression of manifestation in the fourth sephiroth is Geburah, the fifth sephiroth. Geburah is active and attributed to Mars. Like its color red, it means strength or severity. It is the same peaceful lake, but the waves are crashing against the shore churned up by the force of a hurricane.

Geburah is not mercy and union as in Chesed. It is severity and breaking away from things which oppose union (love).

Geburah is also manifested strength and activity called upon while doing calisthenics, for example. As Chesed builds up, Geburah destroys. Like every sephiroth it can be harmful or beneficial; as in the destruction of disease!

Tiphareth

It is said too much mercy is the handwork of a fool; too much severity is the handiwork of a madman. Thus the two balance in the sixth sephirah called Tiphareth, which is harmony, beauty, and equilibrium. Like the sun which is attributed to it, this sephirah is the center of the Tree. Healing is also found here. The sacrificed gods of any religion belong here, including the idea of crucifixion.

By looking at the diagram of the Tree, you will see that Tiphareth is directly under the influence of Kether, above. Therefore, one who attains to it is enabled to know, ("converse"; contact at will) and use Kether's personal power. Such attainment transcends reason. Thus, the all-knowing higher self (Christ-consciousness, Buddhahood, etc.) of Tiphareth is the link to the universal consciousness. The harmony of man and God (the "contact point" between both) is attributed to Tiphareth.

Netzach

The seventh sephirah is called Netzach and represents the senses, or conversely, that which affects the senses. Feeling, such as romantic love, is represented here. This is the sephirah of nature and art. It is the subconscious connection to other people and nature.

Hod

The eighth sephirah is called Hod. It is Netzach's opposite, the intellect. Science, math, and all such matters belong to Hod. It symbolizes reason and data.

Yesod

Again, there must be a balance of the former two sephiroth in order for growth to occur, and the synthesis of these is in the ninth sephiroth called Yesod. It represents the influences that mold the subconscious and how the subconscious acts through the personality.

Yesod means foundation. It is the base (graphically) of what would be a perfectly balanced glyph, were it not for the final sephirah below it.

Yesod is like a funnel; all sephirotic forces must flow through it in order to manifest in the final sephirah. Thus it can be said to represent purification.

Malkuth

Just below Yesod is the final culmination of this transmutation of creative energy into materialization, called Malkuth. This is where manifestation terminates, expressing itself in the physical world, i.e., the world of elements. Malkuth represents the elements, and all physical manifestations occur here. Thus, Malkuth is translated to mean the kingdom because man lives here and it is his home. Basically, Malkuth symbolizes the manifested state of anything. It is the reflection of the spiritual state/Kether.

The Paths On The Tree

The ten sephiroth comprise Creation, while the 22 paths on the Tree are microcosmic phenomena, expressions of the universal macrocosmic sephiroth they connect. In other words, the paths are the phenomena that a person experiences relative to him/ or herself. The sephiroth are manifestations of universal forces, and the paths are the soul's experiences of non-manifested consciousness. The sephiroth are represented by the angels and the paths by the archangels. (God is the Ain and the world of lifeless shells are the Qliphoth.)

To refer to the sephiroth as objective means that man sees them functioning separately from himself. The sephiroth (i.e., severity, mercy, intellect, beauty) do not have the power to control man's soul. Yes, he may be part of the universe, but man has a more developed nature, because his soul has a Will. Soul is superior to the elements. Man was made the dominant species of the world because of his Will, although he often allows the elements to control or affect him. Thus the sephiroth are macrocosmic because they represent elementary forces. (See "The Four Worlds" pg. 55).

Paths are microsocmic because they represent the epitome of natural forces as part of the Will of man. They control the elements. They are subjective because they are a part of man's living experience. Conversely, the elements are only a part of man's bodily experience.

The trumps of the Tarot correspond to and explain the experiences represented by these 22 paths. The 40 "small" cards explain every sephiroth as it acts (or appears) in each of the four worlds.

Enlightenment, in our method, is obtained by attaining to the sephiroth, and then mastering the paths connecting the two sephiroth at each end. "Pathworking" is a popular word today, but know that true pathworking cannot be realized so easily. Attainment may come in time according to the true Will of the individual. Most importantly, know that there is a relationship between man and the universe. Both are subject to certain natural phenomena and forces.

The Four Worlds

The Tree can be divided into four sections from the top down. The first one is the Atziluth, the spiritual world, where the deepest of all vibrations and the perfected part and purpose of anything is found. Next is the creative world, called the Briah. All the emotions or non-intellectual forces occur in the Briah, in preparation for formidable expression in the third world, called Yetzirah. This is the intellectual comprehension of a thing, the idea. The element air is attributed to it (swords in the tarot deck). It is said that this is where the plan of making an idea manifest occurs. Such manifestation occurs in the final physical world called the Assiah. This is the physical aspect of a thing.

Manifested reality exists only in the Assiah, the world of formations. The image of reality that is passed on to the intellect (the Yetzirah) is only that, an image, a representation, not manifested reality itself, but a personal intellectual perception of it. Thus the intellect can create falsehood. So we must project our consciousness into the consciousness of the object itself or bring the object to the reality of our imagination to truly see it.

The Briah, the creative world, is only how one's senses are affected by the senses of reality. The ethereal presence of the reality of the Atziluth is part of the same system as the observer. Thus, that is how we "see," and how we see people's auras not with our eyes.

World:	Atziluth	Briah	Yetzirah	Assiah
Element:	Fire	Water	Air	Earth
Suit In Tarot:	Wands	Cups	Swords	Disks
Court Card:	Knights	Queens	Princes	Princesses
Mode:	Active Male Positive	Passive Female Negative	Active Male Positive	Passive Female Negative
What This Refers To:	Spirit Inception of anything Unseen origins or energies God, Career, Business	Emotions Creativity Desire	Ideas Sickness and Health Depression Measurements	Physical or Manifestation Money
Personification Of Energy Form:	God	ArcAngel	Angel	Distillation into an element
Number	1	2	3	4

So ultimately one must divest oneself of the image or intellectual perception of another that they are their body. This is why preconceived perceptions (i.e. prejudices) are counter to true higher vision or reality. The higher vision allows one to see real differences and know that they are illusions.

A training method for correcting this "false perception" is to perceive things through the eyes of another observer. This should be done regularly, and it will show that the same object or event will be seen very differently by each individual observer. An example of this is a picture of a stone. The picture may be real but the stone is somewhere else. Elementals and other entities use this misrepresentation (deception) method to possess the unknowing through their prejudice.

Qliphoth

Below the Tree of Life is an area called (and filled with) the Qliphoth. They are symbols of lifelessness and they are absent of any speck of life. Not being on the Tree, they could never climb the Tree to attain to unite with God.

Literally called the evil demons, the Qliphoth dwell in the world of shells. It is called the world of shells because the shell represents the absence of life similar to a snail when the animal leaves it and the lifeless shell remains behind.

An evil demon is the uncreated or lifeless part of every aspect (sephirah) on the Tree. Furthermore, the Qliphoth ultimately represent non-growth (which is synonymous with non-change, for growth cannot occur where there is stagnation). Growth can occur through death, which is change. Lifelessness is inertness.

Adaptability is absolutely essential to the magickian! Inertness is the greatest evil he can face! Enemies of a magickian cannot harm one unless they are powerful enough to stop all change from occurring in one's life! Change is life. Thus, inertness is no life. To take it further, then, life is God. Having no life, then the Qliphoth has no soul.

Triangles On The Tree

In the diagram on page 57, you can see three triangles superimposed on the Tree. The top triangle is the Supernal triangle, it is the only upward triangle on the Tree. It is composed of the

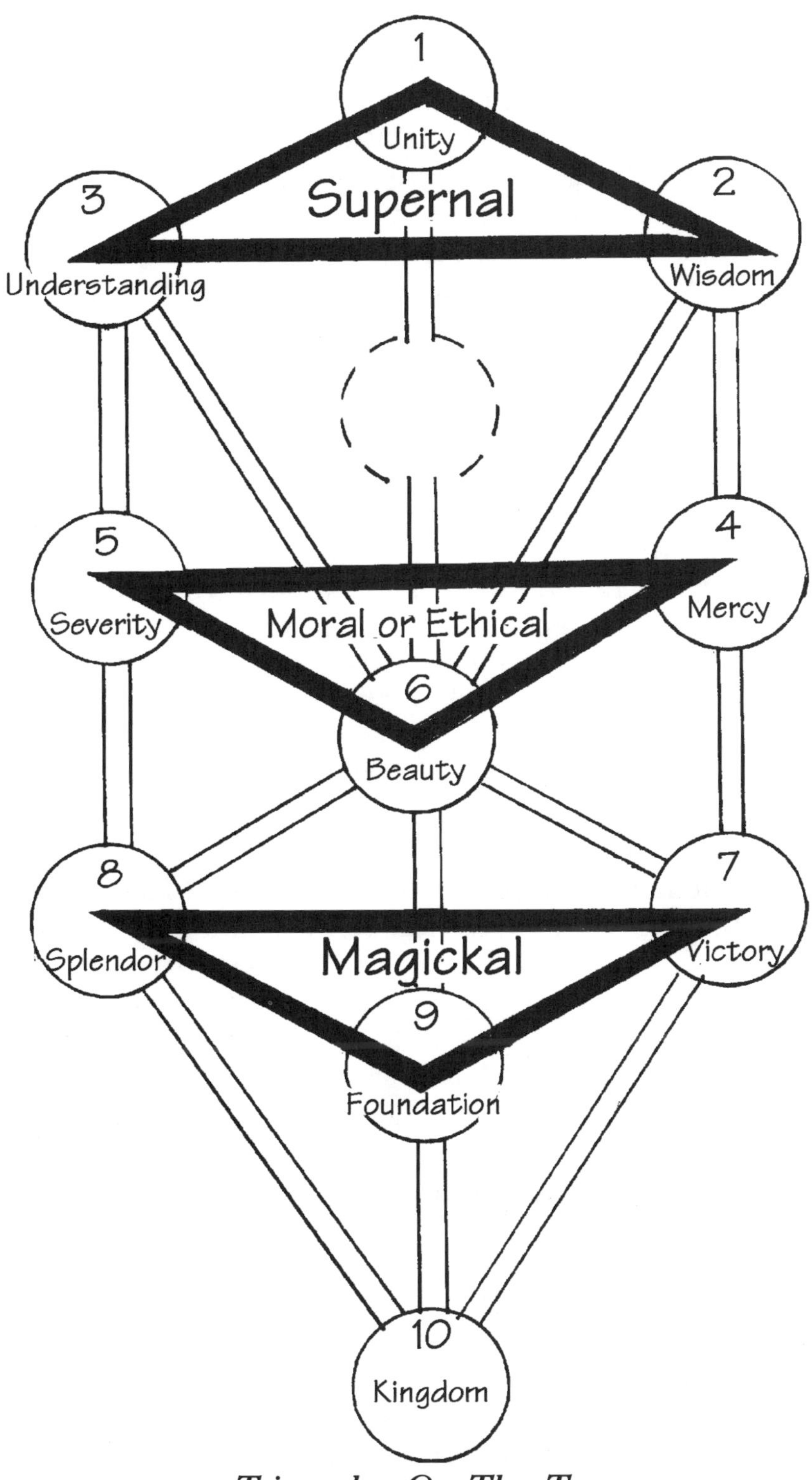

Triangles On The Tree

highest three sephiroth as varying degrees of white. White then "densifies" into grey, which then becomes the all absorbing tone, black. Symbolically, this suggests that the all-emanating Source creates two new variations of itself; opposite and complimentary. These three "supernals" make the first geometrically whole figure, a triangle.

The three sephiroth, Kether (spirit/perfection/unity), Chokmah (wisdom), and Binah (understanding), compose the original and virgin creation; both of the perfected man and anything that one can perceive.

To be spiritually attained to unity with God, one must be truly wise. However to be wise, one must truly understand and conversely to understand one must be truly wise! There cannot be wisdom without understanding, or understanding without wisdom.

In the current human race, souls incarnate by combining with the elements; their physical bodies are man's limitation. For this reason, we can only know of the phenomenon of "the Kether/Unity distillation" when the supernal triangle is expressed in the lower more understandable elements, or when supernal form descends to man's intellectual comprehension.

Through our prism, the white light of the supernal triangle gets refracted and we perceive blue, red, and yellow—the moral or ethical triangle (Chesed, Geburah, and Tiphareth). Its name has become misleading, due to the semantics over ages.

> *To be spiritually attained to unity with God, one must be truly wise.*

In the magickal Qabalah, this second triangle explains the supernal triangle on a lower, more comprehensible level. Man can identify with these "ideas made manifest," and, as human nature is wont to do, "judgments" were assigned to represent these higher actions.

Like the supernal triangle, the three sephiroth of the moral triangle also comprise a harmony of passive receptivity (Chesed, to accept the supernal "distillation"); activity with power (Geburah); and the reflection of a deeper, more complete source (Tiphareth).

The moral triangle is so important because it connects the higher (supernal triangle) to the lower (magickal triangle).

The third triangle is called the magickal triangle. Magick is not the goal; unity with God is the goal. But Magick is the tool for achieving such unity. One's magickal pursuit begins here with Netzach (the sephirah of nature), Hod (the sephirah of intellect and magickal teachings), and Yesod (the sephiroth of one's own subconscious and how it reveals or obscures that which is above).

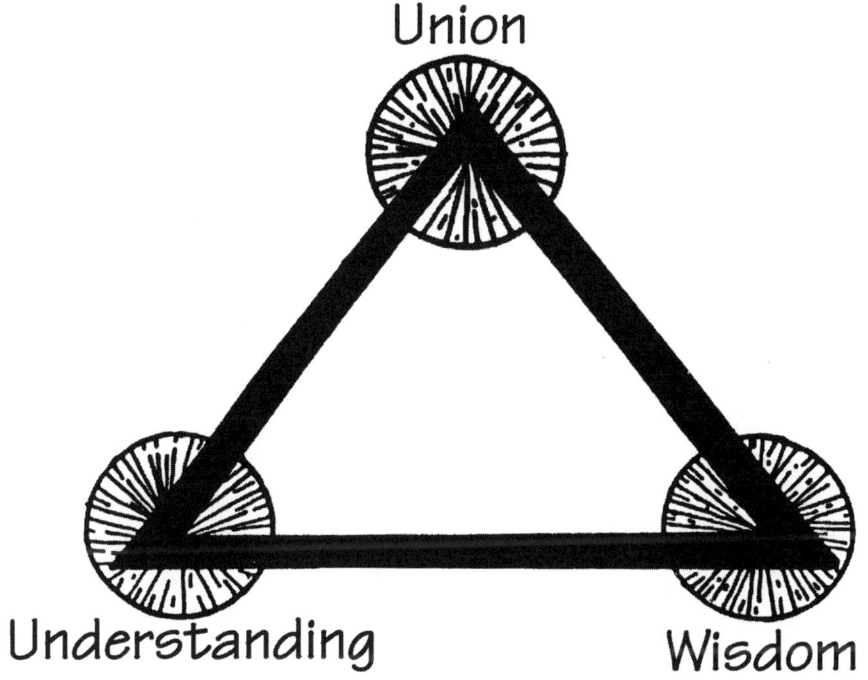

Pythagoras said, "To solve a problem, or answer a question, make a triangle out of it!"

All of these parts of the soul infuse with the elements in the pendant sephirah, Malkuth. When united to the above energies, Malkuth rises up to Kether, its originator.

Pillars On The Tree

Look at the Tree of Life. A very important configuration of three pillars or columns can be visualized(see page 49). By acquainting yourself with the different patterns and configurations on the Tree, you gain a deeper understanding of it.

The "Pillar of Mercy" is the right-hand pillar, formed of Chokmah, Chesed, and Netzach. The "Pillar of Severity" is the left hand pillar, formed of Binah, Geburah, and Hod. The "Pillar of Mildness" is between the two, formed of Kether, Tiphareth, Yesod, and Malkuth.

The right pillar is anabolic (building up); positive; masculine. Its opposite pillar is catabolic (breaking down), negative, feminine. The reconciler between the two is the mysterious "Pillar of Equilibrium" synthesizing the two.

The perfect harmony of both anabolic and catabolic forces (like poles of a battery) is essential to everything in the universe. Either one out of balance is a blind energy or form. All three pillars are equally divine.

Superimposing The Tree On Your Body

It is important to know that the Tree as you are now looking at it, is from an objective perspective. But if you approach it from the inside out and superimpose yourself on the Tree, it becomes subjective and the two sides reverse! That is, the left side of the Tree is on the right side of the body, and visa versa. It's all a matter of whether you are looking in or out. Observing the Tree outwardly is observing the macrocosm. Observing the Tree from the inside (superimposed) would be the microcosm. *Never* is the Tree turned upside-down, however! That is Satanic, *existence before manifestation: the Ain, Ain Soph, and the Ain Soph Aur.*

The Tree of Life (by its ten sephiroth) explains all aspects of anything that is manifested. But what about that which is not manifested? What is on the other side of manifestation, and what is the relationship between the two?

Existence does not have to be manifested to exist. Kether is the source of manifestation and the distillate of non-manifestation. Nothingness is the first mentioned state of non-manifestation. (Bear in mind that manifestation doesn't just mean physical tangibility. Energy is manifested too, yet it is sometimes not tangible. Ideas, emotions, powers, and other things are also manifested.) Nothingness means the absence of manifestation *but* not the absence of existence! This state of nothingness is called the Ain. The Ain is the seed containing the germ from which manifestation may occur. (For example, a woman carries the seed from which the germ of a person—a zygote—may occur).

The mirror image and identical replica of any thing manifested exists in its non-manifested form in a "state" called the Ain Soph. When something exists on the manifested plane it is limited to a certain size, feeling, shape, energy, effect, thought or idea represented in a person's mind, etc. But when something is not yet manifested, it doesn't have the limits of size, feeling, or shape. Thus Ain Soph means "the limitless." Anything can be anything.

Imagine something which exists in the Ain Soph as being given the potential ability or energy to manifest. Imagine a log in a fire. It is matter, yet it gets converted into flame energy. The flame emanates light and heat. If you could film this and play it back in reverse you would have a simple picture of how the non-manifestation of heat/light "condenses" into flame which further transforms into a log. So, something in the Ain Soph that takes on an "enigmatic or vaporous" state is said to be in the Ain Soph Aur. From the Ain Soph Aur come Kether—which is manifested through not yet form which occurs in Chesed; the specific identifiable form occurs in Malkuth. Simply, Ain Soph Aur means "negative light" as if it were a visible light which could condense into manifestation.

This brief explanation attempts to convey one viewpoint of a very abstract topic of the veils of "negative existence." Don't overthink this concept. Keep it simple if you want to eventually be led into understanding it.

One final, more advanced concept: God is perfection. Kether is perfection. Yet, it is manifest. So, God is also non-manifest and exists on the other side of manifestation as do the three veils.

Ancient Egypt

Life in pre-dynastic Egypt revolved around spirituality. The temples were entire cities. It was the first documented scientifically known religion which served as the origin of all others. It is the foundation of the Western Hermetic system.

Prior to the ancient Egyptian civilization, the continent of Atlantis excelled. Before it sank, its people are given signs and warnings to heed, just like the natural disasters, earthquakes, volcanoes, runaway asteroids, and other "anomalies" that are spontaneously occurring today. Some Atlanteans disregarded them, but the wise heeded them and left to settle in other places, especially Egypt.

The hierophant was the dominant figure of pre-dynastic Egypt. The large structures we know today as temples were respectfully reserved for those who were chosen as holy enough to use them. Those who did not meet such high standards would go to smaller chapels in the towns; but each home had a temple which the family enjoyed (as common as today's family entertainment rooms). The Egyptians were so devoted they lived their spirituality everywhere, at all times.

What is commonly not understood about the ancient Egyptians is that although they were monotheistic, they were wise enough to recognize God as having many forms.

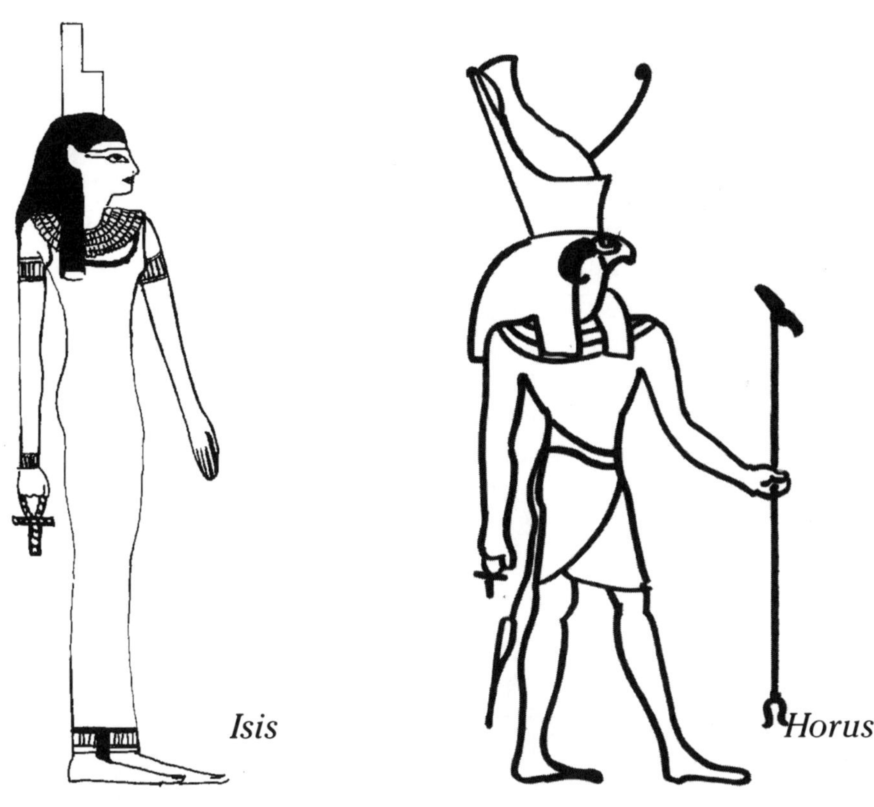

The Gods

Ra can be called the father of the gods, the Creator. He is eternal. All other gods are aspects of Ra. For example, Horus is the forceful side of Ra and Anubis is the protective side of Ra. Often two god-forms were combined into one, or a god-form who changed at different times or places was given different names. Ra in the act of creating anything is called Tem, which means "Ra the creator of Creation." Being the source of gods, Ra is the source of life itself. All the gods and goddesses have a symbol attributed to them. Ra's symbol is the solar disk, the sun. In dynastic Egypt, obliskes were built as his symbol. Queen Hatsepshut was his living daughter.

A very important point to understand is that the ancient Egyptians did not worship the sun itself, but rather the god Ra whom it represents. Accordingly, our High Magick teaches that to master an element or phenomenon, one appeals to the force, the god or the goddess who controls the phenomenon. In other words we do not adore the element or phenomenon itself. For example, for the Nile to rise and fertilize the land, the magickian practicing High Magick prays to the god Hapi, not the river itself. The same goes for the moon, cats, alligators, etc. No ancient Egyptian ever worshipped them as gods (despite what your archaeology and history textbooks say). These Egyptians, as do we, recognize them as symbols of the different powers of the gods and goddesses.

Kephera

Isis is the Mother of all the Egyptian goddesses—all the goddesses are various aspects of her. She gives life to the individual and all of the Creation. She is the mother of Harpocrates (the child God). This first, pre-Christian goddess conceived her child divinely, without conventional physical means. She delivered him similarly. Her husband Osiris was murdered, yet by her Magick she resurrected him. For this, she was taught the words of Magick, by Thoth. She learned the Magick of Ra; how to give life.

All elements have her spirit as their mother— she reveals mysteries to the just. Nothing can grow without her nurturing.

She is said to be the bearer of love and beneficence, yet she has had more trials and tribulations than any other goddess. The loss of her husband and sorrows of her child are the origins of what we call "romance" today. Every tradition that came after the very ancient Egyptians has used her as the role model for a most profound energy that only she can exemplify. She is he epitome of woman and the most graceful of goddesses.

When we think of nature, we think of Isis, being the virgin state of all life. Her sister, Nephthys, is considered "dark," because she makes manifest the Virgin's, unmanifested spirit, but much misunderstanding surrounds her. It is very important to consider Isis and Nephthys as a pair of two complimentary opposites, rather than isolate them in study. The

Nephthys

combination of these two symbolic forces is called Merti. One gives spirit, the other body. Striving to create nothing but form, Nephthys conspired to take the life from the god Osiris, by locking him in a chest to assist in killing him. However, She does protect the organs and the body itself.

Thoth is the early Egyptian god of learning, science, and Magick. Thoth gave the primitive Egyptians technology when they were barely learning how to capture food. Archaeologists concur that these tribe-people mysteriously learned sophisticated mathematics, astronomy, building, speech, and the most intricate hieroglyphics "overnight!"

All education comes under Thoth's domain. The mind is attributed to him. Thoth is the Great Teacher that prepares humans for each approaching aeon so that the incumbent god may readily enter. Thoth provides the magickal words in addition to mathematics and law. He designed and measured the entire universe. He was also called Tahuti by the Egyptians, but later became Hermes to the Greeks, and Mercury to the Romans; thus the name Hermes Trismegistus (Thrice Great) came about.

Thoth (as Hermes) engraved the "Emerald Tablet" which is really made of moldavite. It was discovered by Alexander the Great. Etched upon it is the original alchemical formula from which the popular axiom "As above so below" is derived.

Thoth is responsible for the Great Pyramid. Its designer is thought to be the mysterious Amenhotep, who was said to be a demigod or reincarnation of Thoth. Debate surrounds who or what Amenhotep was, but he did exist and had some form of superhuman power. Scientists today search for his remains. (We are now on the brink of such a discovery. I predict that this discovery will trigger the advent of the apocalypse.)

Thoth

Thoth has the head of an ibis, the bird which is attributed to him. It is easy to see why. This bird will stand for long periods of time on one leg, contemplating. And, although dead ibises were mummified, the early Egyptians did not believe these animals were Thoth, but symbolized him.

Thoth gave words to restore the eye which had been knocked out of Horus. Also when Horus cut his mother Isis's head off, Thoth gave her a cow's head. Thoth (always the measurer) prevented one god from destroying another on several occasions. It was even his duty to avert the destruction of the "dark one", Set, the dark force propagating eternal destruction. He also gave the words to create the universe.

When Horus (son of Osiris) finally captured Set to avenge his father's death, Thoth advised Isis (mother of Horus) to free Set so there would be equilibrium in the universe. Otherwise the universe would have been thrown into a state of imbalance hitherto unknown to humans. We see Thoth is rational, without perturbation. His decisions are impeccable. He weighs and records the deeds of the candidate at the judgment of the deceased and reports them accurately to Osiris.

Since Thoth gives the power to convert the Will to words, the act of speaking is said to be a sacred act, just as sacred as entering a temple and praying. Thus, words are power, though that may be hard to understand because this transformation is not visible.

On the Tree of Life, Thoth is placed in the mercurial Hod.

Osiris is the god that was sometimes called the Black God, God of the Underworld and Judge of the

Osiris

Dead. He rules over death and was a most important object of devotion. (Thus life exists even in death!) He bestows rewards or "punishments" in the after life to those who come before him. It was because Osiris overcame death that he was granted such authority. When He walked the earth, Set, his complimentary brother (nature is always in balance in the Egyptian tradition) Thoth gave Magickal words to Isis teaching her how to resurrect him. The transformed Osiris arose enlightened by the process. (This is the precursor to the story of Christ's resurrection that was to follow thousands of years later.)

It is of utmost importance to understand that Osiris judges not on morals but on the balance or imbalance of the universal forces of the candidate. Serious aspirants who take the opportunities that deity gives them are judged (receive life's circumstances) differently than idle ramblers who chose to reject them. The unfit attract a force represented by Ammit, a monster who devours the heart. Ammit was invincible, ferocious. He stood near Osiris, when judging the dead, waiting for him to condemn those who dwell in illusion and ego instead of reality. Those whom Osiris judges as living in truth, receive the reward of initiation. Thoth recorded the deeds of truth and illusion. These records have become known as the Akashic records.

For further insight to the Egyptian legends, here are a few interpretations to apply when you read the texts:[1]

Dead: Children of the darkness seeking the light. Darkness is ignorance, humans after "the fall," when souls become subordinate to elements (elements are anything without life that can be mistaken for life.) It also represents the candidate seeking enlightenment.

Underworld: Where the dead dwell; going through spiritual practices in preparation for initiation.

Afterlife: Where the aspirant follows the paths to fulfilling karma and transcends mortality.[2] However, if the inertia of stagnation and the lower part of the soul have not been controlled, the enterer will meet nature's "reaction"! Nature reacts mechanically; it does not discriminate.

Evil: Not a moral concept, but that which restricts one's Will and that which separates humans from God.

Horus takes many forms, but mainly he is the warrior god who avenges Osiris's (his father) death so that light may reign. Horus does this not out of emotion; instead His "job" is to make sure each soul defeats the taker of life. Technically, Horus is the reconciler. His mother was Isis, and as a child he was called Harpocrates.

Anubis is the watcher of the gods. Jackals symbolized a force called Anubis. They are acutely aware. Anubis watched over those who undertook initiation. He is also the god who Embalms—secures the deceased for their journey into the world of the dead and keeps their souls from invasions from the living or dead. He is the *son* of Nephthys.

Kephera is the god that represents the midnight sun

---

1. The Hermetic path teaches never to take any holy book literally.
2. Living directed by circumstances instead of being master of all personal phenomena.

which never dies but only goes onto another part of the world. Kephera is symbolized by the beetle or scarab. Kephera is particularly important in this tradition when the sun is overcome by darkness by setting early, after the autumnal equinox and into the winter as the darkness grows. Conversely, his prominence over the dark winter nights also invokes this Kephera light.

The Beetle is sacred and was said to have been self-propagating; also it lays its eggs in its own dung, then rolls them in the sand from East to West (the same direction as the sun) until they hatch!

The lion-headed goddess Sekhmet is the scorching aspect of nature's forces. Here is her amazing story:

As Egyptians embraced more rationale, they started to stray from the spiritual roots that made them and their society so fruitful. They took spirituality for granted. Enlightenment took a back seat to more sensual endeavors. People became debauched. Ra saw this and, to save his creation, was forced to order Sekhmet to infiltrate and eliminate "the adversaries." She did so successfully but, as is her nature, her thirst for blood would not be quenched until all were slain. Ra respected Sekhmet, and still granted her great power over humanity. Yet he had to stop her slaughtering somehow. He had red dye and beer poured into the Nile. He intended to trick Sekhmet into believing it was the blood of all the people. On the day of his trick, she went to the waters of the Nile and saw they were reddened with "blood." Thinking she had slain all the people, Sekhmet relaxed and celebrated by drinking beer and became intoxicated to the point of losing her power of vengeance. Thus, the people who were true-of-heart survived.

Lioness Sekhmet, therefore had no more power to hunt and kill. Ra summoned her and said, "You come in peace, sweet one. Peace be with you and a new name. No longer are you Sekhmet the slayer: You are Hathor the Lady of Love. Yet your power shall be even greater than it was—for the passion of love shall be stronger than the passion of hate and all shall know love, and all shall be your victims!"

Nuit is the Egyptian goddess that symbolizes the sky. Her hands and feet touch her husband, Seb (the earth god), by bowing. This benevolent mother goddess would meet the

Nuit and Seb

seeker face to face and protect him or her on his or her journey. She is infinite space. She is the recognition of the individual Will of every person. She brings down ultimate understanding to her followers.

One might think that some of the legends of ancient Egypt were merely hallucinations of fairy tales of a primitive society. However, the Egyptians were wise, and their tales were not shallow rhetoric. When they first received their wisdom, they were living in harmony with nature. They put spirit ahead of all else. They believed that every act should be Magickal. They left behind legends of their powerful gods which reveal the steps to enlightenment. They remain in the amazing ruins and writings that continue to be uncovered.

The Curse Of Tutankhamen:
A Documentary

Tut was an inconsequential pharaoh who took the throne in about 1334 B.C. Much of the greatness of Egypt passed thousands of years before, however the tales of his artifacts made him famous. The history-making excavation made such an impact that tourists began to gather around the tomb. Lord Carnarvon, an Englishman, was the agent in unearthing Tut's peaceful tomb. He did not suspect his involvement in this project would lead to his demise.

His health required that he go to a warm, dry climate. He chose Egypt (or did Egypt choose him?). There he met Howard Carter, known to be unusually driven by his colleagues. Carter was fired from the civil service in Egypt for his rudeness to a superior. He stayed on in Egypt, obsessively seeking Tut's tomb for fifteen years, and trying to persuade Lord Carnarvon to provide the funds, which he eventually supplied.

In November 1922, the tomb's entrance was discovered. Its doors had protective religious seals, warning intruders that they would suffer the penalties of the gods if they broke the seals and entered the tomb.

Carter wired Lord Carnarvon of this successful find and asked him to come and join him in opening the tomb, thus defying the will of the priests who sealed it.

If this first seal were not enough, Tut bore another warning to intruders around his neck—an elaborate gold pectoral of the vulture goddess, Nekbeht. Additionally, a tablet, missing today under unusual circumstances, again warned those who disturbed the peace of Tut's tomb they would meet with death.

Earlier tomb robbers had left evidence of their presence but had not dared to break the seals.

Carter removed and catalogued Tut's treasures. Lord Carnavon took his share home but, as soon as he arrived, a fever which developed strangely from an ordinary mosquito bite took his life. The reports listed his death officially as pneumonia, but the world discounted this report, and some called it a cover-up. Public opinion was that by disturbing Tut's tomb he received the Magickal punishment, since all the lights in Cairo went out at exactly the minute he died. In England, his dog Susie got up on her hind legs, let out a horrified yelp, and rolled over dead at that very same minute!

Lord Carnarvon's death was only the first in a series of accursed and extraordinary deaths. Carter's assistant, Richard Bethel, was next to go; he died suddenly of a circulatory collapse. Bethel's father, Lord Westbury, although reputed to be mentally stable by those who knew him almost all of his life, killed himself. The chief Egyptologist who was supposed to be in charge of bringing these artifacts to the Louvre and the Metropolitan Museum died immediately after arriving at the tomb. Jay Gould, the American financier and contributor of the expedition who had the special privilege of being among the first to see the tomb, also died suddenly. By that time, twenty-two deaths had been directly attributed to the curse.

An American artist, Joseph Lindon Smith, while copying the wall paintings of the discovery, decided to dispel the curse by putting on a play which used ancient Egyptian rituals. At the final dress rehearsal, however, at the very moment Akenaton's prayer of overcoming the "cursing gods" was being spoken,[1] an unheard of, history-making gigantic hailstorm erupted!

Akenaton's denial of the old gods was again unsuccessful. The Egyptian's who were hired to help with the production claimed the gods were "throwing stones" at them, so the rehearsal had to

> *...twenty-two deaths had been directly attributed to the curse.*

be aborted. The actor and actress who played Akenaton and his mother had the same dream that night: they dreamt that they stood in a temple of Amon Ra and his statue came to life and struck them. The actress dreamt she was struck across the stomach; the other dreamt he was struck violently across the face. Within forty-eight hours the actress was in surgery undergoing an emergency abdominal operation; at the same

---

1. Akenaton opposed the religion of Tut, and for a while popularized his own religion. He died after only seventeen years of his reign, and Tut's religion once again ruled. All the status of Akenaton and mentions of his name were destroyed.

time, the actor developed what doctors called the worst case of sight-attacking trachoma ever seen in Europe.

It has been documented that every single person associated with the production was struck with some illness, varying from minor to critical, within the same forty-eight hours! The only person involved in the project whose fate was still pending was Howard Carter. For the rest of Carter's life, all those around him died, were stricken by illness, or had misfortunes. In the midst of the Tut discovery, he came under governmental prosecution and was legally barred from going near the tomb; the government claimed it wanted only serious archaeologists to study the tomb. Carter appealed this decision, and protracted legal battles ensued. His world had collapsed!

Carter had lengthy problems in and out of court. His obsession with opening the tomb was replaced by the necessity to survive those he had defiled by claiming that his discovery entitled him to more than his share. When he was finally allowed by the government to recover his precious archaeological treasures, all the unguents which sealed them had dissolved, destroying their prized inner contents!

His variety of personal tragedies and failures devastated him. He was called the "master of the dead" (as well as being the violator). It was documented that Lord Carnavon's fatal mosquito bite scarred Carter's left cheek. Tut's mummy had the same mark in exactly the same place! Both his first and last names have six letters (Howard Carter). He died in 1939 at the age of sixty-six during the vernal equinox, when life is supposed to come to man. Some claim that he was a desecrating aspect of spirituality, thus systemizing 666 mathematically. According to numerology this number symbolizes Satan, or the evil aspect.

Carnavron's supporting partner Woolf Joe, and the x-ray team of Sir Archibald Douglas Reid and Frederick Raleigh, died on their way to the site. The list of misfortune and tragedy that befell those who followed Carter closely in the project goes on. Nature does not discriminate: If the creator says that you will be electrocuted if you switch a light on when standing in a pool of water, no matter how benevolent your intent is, you will be electrocuted. Those who tamper with higher forces without the guidance of a master, ignorantly thinking they can't get hurt because they mean well, or challenge those forces for any egotistical reason, beware—those same forces that created you can turn you can turn you to cinders in a second! Thus the gods of ancient Egypt punished those who violated the protection of Tut's tomb.[2] It should be noted, however, that the discovery was instrumental in keeping the light of the Egyptian gods, which will burn forever, in the world. The gods indeed work in mysterious ways.

2. The original movie of *The Mummy* with Boris Karloff contained some valid information, woven into this Hollywood novelty. Its creators knew something about the esoteric land its rituals.

Tarot

The tarot is Qabalah in pictures. So, see the chapter on Qabalah. The magickal (spiritual) forces and phenomenon of the self and the universe are symbolized in one complete book given to man by the ancient Egyptian god Thoth. This book is called tarot. Its pictures have been discovered on the ancient temple walls of the Egyptians.

Students of Magick were taught that these images could be meditated upon to reveal what influences and energies would be present at any given time and place; the birth of forecasting using tarot symbols had begun.

Whether you use the tarot to unravel the General Universal Laws, or to see what forces lie surround you, proper use will sharpen your senses, uncover deep parts of your self, and align you to a portion of nature.

It is important to learn to use the cards as focal points for meditation/skrying. Thus the cards are only tools that open the centers of the higher self that will reveal certain knowledge. Remember, they in themselves are powerless pieces of cardboard. The power lies in the reader's ability to unite with universal symbols that triggers higher functions. You, as the Tarot reader, are capable of unlocking the answer to anything you want to know. Also, by placing the cards into predesigned arrangements, you can learn how the energies symbolized in the tarot work. This understanding of the unseen forces in essential to learning the language of the tarot. It is also a valuable and essential training method for developing your intuition.

The Trumps
Know that there are 22 trumps or major keys at the beginning of the deck. They represent Superior Forces, not affected by, but above the elements and planets. To understand the

tarot fully, you must understand Qabalah. The Qabalist knows the symbols of the tarot in his or her understanding. The trumps are the paths and are objective. They represent the experiences of nature, the divine, the macrocosmic. They are every phenomenon of the universe. By determining their efforts, the aspirant can unravel their influence on him or herself.

These Trumps pertain to spirit: Fool, Magus, Empress, Hierophant and Chariot.

These Trumps pertain to individuality: Priestess, Emperor, Lovers, Lust and Hermit.

The "higher" reflection of man: Fortune, Adjustment, Hanged Man.

These pertain to personality: Death, Art, Devil, Tower, Star, Moon, Sun, Aeon and Universe.

Broadly speaking, spirit is the whole being, the soul (sometimes called the "God"-part of the person).

Individuality refers to the souls true, natal identity as given by God which has not

The book which explains nature and man (The Book of Thoth, i.e. Tarot) shows the magickian as director of the elements which have no divine reasoning power.

been influenced by the will of other people or experiences (i.e., the true self, the original state of man; although this is not Godhood, it is free of distractions and distortions which misdirect one from the true original purpose. (See page 11 "The Will"). Personality is how you express your soul in the outer world, (i.e. the reflection of your soul on this side of manifestation).

By studying the tarot in relation to one's self, many great personal attainments can be made. Study each card individually.

All of these cards are doubly dignified. That is, they can be constructive or destructive depending on their placement and surrounding factors.

The Court Cards

The "creative source" is symbolized by the Trumps. Four elements characteristic of this creative source being expressed are also recognized. These can be corporeal and characteristic of nature. They also represent the four planes: spirit, emotion, intellect, matter, (as taught in Qabalah). These forces are personified to make their behavior in manifestation more understandable. They are given to humanity to help us understand things pertinent to our development. They are: fire as the wands which represent the spiritual plane including

> *Every element manifests as either a divine source, a sensation, a thought, or physical matter.*

activity and causation; water as the cups which represents the emotional plane and includes creativity, receptivity, the first state of perception before formulation of thought. It is creative, rather than formulated, just the sense of something where the subconscious is ignorant of that which is seen; air as the swords which represent the mental plane and is purely intellectual made up of formulated regimens of plans and is oblivious of unseen things; and earth as the disks which represents the physical plane which is manifestation which completion as the final result.

Every element manifests as either a divine source, a sensation, a thought, or physical matter. Thus there are, respectively, a knight, queen, prince, and princess within each suit.

These elements expressed in their four characteristics comprise the sixteen court card combinations.

From here they make themselves more known, definable, visible, and controllable in existence as natural elemental forces to be used by man in the next principle.

The Small Cards

These subjective and personal depictions of the events of humanity are called lesser keys, minors, small cards, etc. They are the aces through the tens of each suit. The ten sephiroth on the Tree of Life correspond to the ten cards of each suit of the tarot. The aces represent the Kether of the element, i.e., the seed or root. In other words, it is the potential but not manifestation of the element, like a seed is potentially a tree. Existence occurs on all 4 planes (worlds). So each plane is represented in the "Lesser Keys" of the Tarot as a suit.

For example, the 4 of swords (4th state, Chesed) would be the mercy and benevolence of the mind/intellect (swords). You can see why this card is titled "truce"; truce within ones self or with other events. It symbolizes a compassionate order in the intellectual world (plane), free from disorder of disagreement.

Knowing that the suits are the planes of existence, and that the sephirah represent a certain energy or "states" that vibrates to a corresponding number (ie. Kether = 1); you can superimpose these "states" of existence within every plane, and apply them to the "small cards" in the Tarot.

Here is a guide:

1st state: origin; possibility of manifesting in other ways (The Aces are a root or seed, the incomplete base of the element.)

2nd state: wisdom of self or phenomenon (The two's are the identity of the element.)

3rd state: Understanding of what wisdom or phenomenon is. (The threes are how man visualizes these forces of the twos.)

4th state: Mercy—higher love (The fours being the abstract idea of the element into comprehensible form.)

5th state: Shear power (The fives are the comprehensible energies behind the element.)

6th state: Harmony (The sixes are the balance and higher use of the elements virtue.)

7th state: Instincts (The sevens show the "feeling" and reaction produced by the element.)

8th state: Knowledge (The eights are the observable knowledge of the element.)

9th state: The conversion of "that which is above" to "that which is manifested". (The nines show how each element will be naturally expressed in the mundane kingdom where man dwells.)

10th state: The physical reflection of that which is divine. (The tens show how the separated element manifests itself. Remember that manifestation is only one part of a whole. Herein lies a step towards perfection. . .it can transmute from the 10th to the 1st, the base returning again to the divine.

This is the simple system of the Qabalah from which the cards were designed. One cannot know the cards unless one comprehends the Tree of Life, and vice versa. To separate these two studies is erroneous.

The mastery of the Tarot is, therefore, abstract if approached without wisdom.

A Condensed Spiritual Guide To The Trumps

FOOL The idea of unaltered, independent energy; rational or irrational; fresh or foolish.

MAGUS The idea of controlling one's own life according to the laws of the universe.

PRIESTESS The idea of receptivity; opening to intuitive understanding.

EMPRESS The idea of expressing an intent.

EMPEROR The idea of mastery of an intent, active as opposed to the passivity of Empress.

HIEROPHANT The idea of the expounding of mysteries; the link between Creator and creation, a way.

LOVERS The idea of extremes uniting and complementing, rather than changing or conflicting each other.

CHARIOT The idea of anything directing or guiding itself.

LUST The idea of strength conquering weakness.

HERMIT The idea of inspiration or wisdom raising that which is lower within itself, to eventually become higher.

FORTUNE The idea of fruition of manifestation.

ADJUSTMENT The idea of mystical equilibrium.

HANGED MAN The idea of sacrificing the ego and

discovering the inner self.

DEATH The idea of transformation of any kind, changing from one state to another.

ART The idea of creating a higher effect.

DEVIL The idea of complete manifestation unbalanced and with no comprehension of any other plane.

TOWER The idea of destroying the unfit to rebuild.

STAR The idea of divine and Magickal assistance; hope.

MOON The idea of sublime reflection of an origination; sometimes no more than reflection when actual is required.

SUN The idea of health and epitome of consolidation and exertion.

AEON The idea of fulfillment of potential.

UNIVERSE The idea of synthesis; final distillation and connection to the source.

The wise person knows that every trump is double aspected. It has a positive and negative side and can be influenced by surrounding tarot cards or where it appears.

A Magickian's Concise Guide To The Court Cards And Minor Arcanum

Knight of Wands—Active, fiery and forceful. Needs great composure. Confident, intent and directed.

Queen of Wands—Intent and forceful but introspective. Aware of herself. Proud and touchy.

Prince of Wands—Quick, youthful, vigorous. Forceful but indecisive because he sees all the alternatives. Volatile.

Princess of Wands—Sensuous and whimsical. Clever, self-centered or spoiled or devious.

Ace of Wands—Root of energy distilling into matter. Energy of expansion, such as the act of creation.

2 of Wands—Chokmah of the wand (Will). Conquering by force for good. Identity. Sometimes home or self.

3 of Wands—Force given to a body to do its will. Thus the title on the card is virtue as pristine force uninfluenced by other elements.

4 of Wands—The other 3 wands being manifested, this one is completion. Success of will/purpose.

5 of Wands—Geburah of fire, just a active force; unbalanced forming nothing. But strife of evil is good.[1]

6 of Wands—Balance of power; harmony of all forces. Provides good by its delicate strength and wisdom.

7 of Wands—Use of lesser forces; random assertion; poor direction but good intent and efforts.

8 of Wands—Mercurial fire, i.e.; direct and swift action. Energy such as lightning, electricity, etc.

9 of Wands—A firm foundation for energy to use; well directed energy, any intent or action has everything it needs.

10 of Wands—Confined energy; restriction; self-centeredness lacking power or knowledge of anything else.

Knight of Cups—Uses passiveness and charm well; emotionally unstable; sensitive; ruled by emotions.

Queen of Cups—Extremely sensitive; can't see herself through influences and reactions; dainty; reflective.

Prince of Cups—"Scorpio-like"; active by secrecy; silent power; not motivated by conscience; sincere.

Princess of Cups—Utilization of Briah; sensuous; sanguine; undemonstrative; gentle; intangible.

Ace of Cups—Root of water; unformulated; receptive; creates from the native source.

2 of Cups—Union by recombining separations; above separateness; love in all aspects.

3 of Cups—Receptivity into form; receives all things.

4 of Cups—Luxury for good or evil; there is so much, its management is the focal point.

5 of Cups—Pleasure upset; beauty overcome by force; power made passively impotent; disappointment.

6 of Cups—Balance and beauty of all senses; no obstructions but enjoyment.

7 of Cups—Overindulgence of senses; blindness to the obvious; dependence on illusory fulfillment.

8 of Cups—Stagnation; lack of senses; sterility due to inactivity.

9 of Cups—Stable emotions; no imbalances; proper use of water[2] yielding happiness.

10 of Cups—The chalices are filled to satisfaction; no room for anything else; slight activity can spill their contents.

---

1. Strife is a weakened deprived state. So when evil is so debilitated, this is a good condition.
2. Water= Briah (emotions, creativity, desire, love, art, socialaity, etc. See page 54).

Knight of Swords—Causes movement where there should be stillness; clever; inspired but impulsive.
Queen of Swords—Clarity; destroys intellect; sees all; well—planned; enforces justice; graceful bodily control.
Prince of Swords—Must plan for every act; usually to much for use; all idea—no action; rational; malleable.
Princess of Swords—Materializes ideas; vengeful; can manipulate or balance all; thus doesn't conform comfortably.
Ace of Swords—Root of air and consciousness; base of intellectual formation; omnidirectional.
Two of Swords—Peace after conflict; change of status; placid idea; all forces equalized.
3 of Swords—Sorrow of the universe, usually. Perversion; im balance of all—consuming receptivity reducing to form; inevitable loss of original ideal without purpose.
4 of Swords—Chesed (compassion) reconciles and equili-brates all perfectly; allows no assertiveness; acquiesces.
5 of Swords—Geburah's force blindly slashing instead of thinking; allows no peace; uses any unscrupulous means.
6 of Swords—Proper balance of all the above for productiv-ity, allowing the higher forces to operate.
7 of Swords—Frustration; only success would have been appeased; leads to further consequences.
8 of Swords—Too many ideas, all conflicting; search for "all sides" interferes.
9 of Swords—Subconscious instincts running rampant regardless of compassion; nothing humane.
10 of Swords—So much reason that it is literally insane; logic over reason, judgement, feeling, life.
Knight of Disks—Considers without action; looks ahead but priority is what's in front of him; can't take advantage of opportunity.
Queen of Disks—Also looks but is passive; considers every-thing but inactivity allows it to all dry up. Does only what she knows.
Prince of Disks—Slow, strategic, practical; reacts after he decides; cautious; not easily moved by others.
Princess of Disks—Lowest part of earth; always gets benefit from probing deeply, not perceptively or analytically;

a receptacle.

Ace of Disks—Root of matter, but not matter itself; eclipse; spirits descent to manifestation.

2 of Disks—Change; Universe must always change for harmony.

3 of Disks—That which functions by Will; all parts working cooperatively; desired process occurring.

4 of Disks—Power, fortification, endurance; consolidation of resources; inflexible. Strong in design only.

5 of Disks—Weight of self—inflection (worry) by too much consideration of matter and force towards goal.

6 of Disks—Harmonizing, consolidation of all the elements to work under Will, naturally; balanced unity.

7 of Disks—Material has degenerated and as effort is made in one place, it neglects another; full failure.

8 of Disks—A calm, stable prudence; matter slowly accrued, not like seven of Disks (gluttonous); slow growth.

9 of Disks—Fulfillment in everything; all comes to one who spiritually approaches desire for gain.

10 of Disks—Malkuth of Assiah, i.e., most manifestation of material, for good or evil.

> *The tarot is a doorway into the soul.*

Becoming Skilled In Interpreting The Tarot

A good Tarot reading should contain the following:
1) Expertise! When you have been taught tarot properly by your teacher, you then depend on the higher forces to guide you during the interpretation. Abide by Their advice! Don't challenge or manipulate them to give you the answer that you want.

2) Stillness of mind! If you are not objective, you'll "project" your thoughts (rather than impressions) into the cards. If you are scattered, you will block higher knowledge from op-

erating through your intellect. (The reader must be versed in contacting the higher force.)

3) Intuition is the key. Never refer to books for an interpretation. The tarot is psychic, not academic. You must feel your specific answers. The books don't know your specific questions!

4) Answers that are general, vague, philosophical, or rhetorical are common among unskilled practitioners. Such responses do not answer the question. The true Tarot reader must be able to go out on the limb and be specific! Detailed answers are much more helpful than hedging around the question. Also, the reader must have learned the art of being spe-

> *Tarot mastery is not computerlike memorization.*

cific with what he wants to know when asking the question. The asking phase is as important as the answering phase.

The individual tarot cards have a myriad of definitions by many authorities. Within each explanation is woven their own perception, knowledge, research, viewpoint and understanding of themselves and their teachers or sources; multiplied in seventy-eight different directions, one for each card.

The more one formally studies tarot, the more of an intellectual operation and the less an intuitional one it becomes. Tarot mastery is not computerlike memorization.

It is important to remember that the purpose of learning Tarot is to understand the energies of the universe and the soul. These seventy-eight symbols in all of their combinations teach the aspirant. The fact that they could reveal influences operating at any given time and place is secondary; it serves to open the way to your own higher facilities.

The tarot is a doorway into the soul. Therefore a Tarot reader and querent openly expose their life essence to each other, unless the reader has certain knowledge and skills to avoid this!

The Hierophant is taught how to properly read cards for others, while the aspirant is advised *not* to read another person's soul energy (i.e. Tarot) because:

a) it serves no purpose, the aspirant usually reads cards for people to inflate his own ego.

b) it creates aura links. Energy leakage is a common risk.[1] Also the danger of malevolent or life seeking beings exists where the life force is extended between one individual and another. (see The Aura pg. 131)

c) The reader is putting the other person's soul in their hands and therefore no allowance can be made for mistakes. The karmic responsibility of being 100% right 100% of the time can only be undertaken by an Adept.

---

1. Those who know readers who tap the resources of the soul are familiar with how quickly their life force dissipates; the burnout occurs in 2-5 years.

Spiritual Astrology

Astrology is a spiritual art. It is not matching academic numbers to a directory. No book contains specifics about any one individual. Interpreting a chart is a psychic process. Accurate and usable interpretation depends on how intuitive the astrologer is. No computer can delve beyond superficial astronomy.

Astrology examines the microcosm and macrocosm...you and the universe. Contrary to popular belief, the stars and planets have no effect on us. Instead, they are manifestations of hidden, more divine energies that are operating. I call the symbols in the skies "signatures" of the Creator intended for man's use; like iron, herbs, and the winds.

Your horoscope is a kind of blueprint that plots the influences present at the moment of birth, that will continue to surround you throughout your life. The horoscope shows the conditions you are going to meet in life. It shows what can happen, not what must happen. Thus, it advises ways to change anything, by your foreknowledge. There is an old saying that says "the stars impel...they do not compel."

> *No computer can delve beyond superficial astronomy.*

Your astrological chart shows the sky as it appeared at the time and place of your birth, when your soul chose to manifest on this plane of existence.

The zodiac is a belt through which the planets move. Essentially, it is divided into 12 houses. They contain every aspect of your life. The signs are constellations that move about the zodiac. The planets are affected by the signs they're in. The signs and planets move through the 12 non-moving demarcations (houses.) Such signs, movements, and positions reveal the composition of your soul and your purpose as well as that which you must learn to be a complete person.

But that is only where the process starts. There are a multitude of considerations to search for in the chart: rising sign, zenith, majorities of signs and houses of a particular nature (such as element, gender, polarity, activity method of expression or experience), release points and other Arabian parts (synthetic points between planetary configurations), groupings by hemisphere and quadrant, retrogrades (planets optically appearing to go backwards from earth's perspective) interceptions (again the perspective of Earth "hiding" signs and planets), patterns formed by planets (crosses, etc.), single planets conspicuous by their isolation, omissions of any of the above as they would appear in the chart ("holes"), aspects between planets, ruling planets' misplacements, focal points and a hundred or more other components.

The use of astrology is documented throughout history. Today especially, astrology is used by concerned individuals as well as by governments and corporations. It has been used successfully by businesses to chart the inception of their business to maximize success, or using "progressions" and "transits" to make important decisions. Actors, playwrights, musicians, athletes, gardeners, etc. have attributed their success to the adherence of astrological forecasts. The silent use of astrology by governments, religions, corporations, etc., is more prevalent today than ever before.

Your astrological wheel is literally a picture of your soul! It is very personal and must be kept and used accordingly.

Using Astrology For Growth

Why use astrology? To find out your strengths and weaknesses; influences that will appear and that which will never manifest.

Casting a natal birthchart is recommended for you own insight towards magickal knowledge of the self. The natal chart is the way you chose to live in this world, while your progressed chart is how you (prenatally) chose to arrange certain events that will take place during your lifetime. Astrology is, therefore, actually "growth." You chose all that your chart(s) reveals for your karmic lessons. They are pictures of your life; characterizing the whole duration (natal chart) and what will occur and how it will affect you at any given time (progressed chart) i.e., being in the "right" (or "wrong") place at the "right" or "wrong" time.

Study this picture of your soul to see where you have strayed and where you have followed your course. Understand why important differences between your chart and your circumstances in life have occurred. In humanistic astrology, the counselor would direct you to discover more about yourself by advising you to be more self-aware;

> *Often people see unfavorable parts of their chart and get unduly alarmed.*

then self-examining your views of what really exists instead of how you rationalize what "should" exist. The two could be different. If so, why? For example, why do you fail at something which is naturally easy for you? Or vice versa. What adaptations and influences have shaped your life? In the search for the true Will we cannot overlook certain factors that may have distorted certain natural birth traits. Thus to begin to work towards your life's purpose you begin to eliminate that which is not the true you. From early childhood on, one is always subjected to influences and standards of other people such as peers, role models, media, teachers, parents, trauma, etc.

Often people see unfavorable parts of their chart and get unduly alarmed. They decide that they are destined to a horrible life when, in fact, they may train to reshape their life. Difficult aspects can be adapted to and overcome, using the proper direction.

If you do not know how to construct a chart yourself, get a natal chart made for your birth. (You will need to know your exact time and place of birth.) They can be obtained inexpensively from many occult shops. However, never allow a computer to interpret a chart for you! This must be done by you. A computer can only add and subtract the mathematical erection. It will however give you the number of degrees between planets.

Here are the basics for the synthesis of your natal chart:

1. Look for the sign the sun is in. This tells you your natural purpose (the sun being the individual personality).

2. Look at the rising sign (the sign which is on the first house cusp). The rising sign is how you appear to the world, by your personality.

3. See what sign the moon is in. It shows your emotions and how you respond and create.

An astrological chart is divided into 12 segments called houses. The first house begins at the left horizontal line. The second one is below in a counterclockwise direction. The houses, though, never move. They are merely divisions of the map of the sky (the chart).

The houses have often been called the fields of experience, telling you that any planet or sign that is in the house will be experiences of that house.

Signs show how man's characteristics (traits) manifest themselves. As the earth rotates on its axis, the sky appears to move. Thus a new sign of the zodiac rises over the horizon every two hours.

It is fair to say that the house represents how you relate to a given area of life in general. The house and its corresponding sign (i.e., 1st and Aries) have the same properties, yet the sign is the impersonal experience of that event.

4. The midheaven is the 10th house cusp, the vertical cusp dividing the 9th and 10th houses. See what sign goes over it. Look for planets that are within one degree of it. The midheaven shows the power you will actually have and your position in the world. It is not how you project yourself however; that is represented by the ascendant.

5. Determine if the signs with the planets in them have something in common. For example, are they mostly fire? Or are they predominantly the "cardinal" signs? Are the majority positive? Examine the quadrants especially in relation to planets that occupy them. Look for planetary groupings (a "seesaw" for instance) and for formations such as "cross," "T-

square," "yod," etc. Groupings and formations are things that require astrological training. This goes for looking for stelliums and singletons also.

6. Look at the planets in the signs. The planet takes on the character of the sign it is in. This will then tell you how to use the planets in each house.

7. The planets in the houses show you how to approach each house, bearing in mind the influence given to each planet by the sign it is in. The dignity of every planet will be examined as well. Dignity is if a planet has a particular assignment to a sign. The categories of dignities are Ruler, Exaltation, Fall, Detriment, or Strong. We can also say the planet shows you how to express the qualities and properties of the house.

8. Look at the aspects. These are the angles between planets and are as follows:

Conjunction—two planets close enough to be in the same place. It is a blending of the both energies into one which is either favorable and unifying or adverse and binding.

Square—two planets approximately 90 degrees apart. This induces conflict. If you are able to overcome the obstacles it shows, this leads to success. If you shirk the responsibility of dealing with it, failure is the result.

Opposition—80 degrees (approximately) apart. A tug of war between two facets of your life requiring adapting. These are the major aspects. Other aspects are considered minor. They are:

Sextile—60 degrees (approximately); Opportunity and ease of communication with diverse contacts.

Trine—120 degrees (approximately) apart; Gives hope, optimism, peace and joviality, The angle of an aspect does not have to be exact. The orb of influence is the number of degrees that a planet exerts its influence in the event that the angle is a few degrees larger or smaller.

Signs Of The Zodiac

Like the Tarot, astrological symbolism conveys wisdom of the meanings of things. This wisdom is the true identity or essence of various forces and forms depicted clearly and objectively.

This astrological symbolism is popularly known today for divination purposes. Rarely is it considered anything deeper.

An astrological sign represents a characteristic found within mankind and the creation. It is an archetypal form. They are:

ARIES: Will, being, consciousness, self-projection, health.

TAURUS: Self-exertion, material substance.

GEMINI: Mind, personality formation.

CANCER: Growth through personality, home, sensitivity, operating base in general.

LEO: Self expression and creativity, pleasure.

VIRGO: Detail, serving and devotion, self-judgement.

LIBRA: Human interchange, relationships.

SCORPIO: Sex, death, occultism, regeneration.

SAGITTARIUS: Synthesizing, philosophy, abstract mind.

CAPRICORN: Quality and quantity of social position, politics and social systems but not institutions.

AQUARIUS: Science, music, native genius, humanitarianism and collective ideas.

PISCES: Self-redemption, self-undoing, psychism, mysticism, unconscious, return to native state, institutions.

Planets

By grasping the Tree of Life, one can make certain associations to the planets. Such comprehension is more valuable than any astrology book. However, here are some attributions of the planets:

SUN: Individuality ("spirit"). Healing. Self-mastery. Vitality. Authority. Beauty.

MOON: Emotions. Subconscious. Receptivity. Link from matter to spirit. The manner in which spirit expresses itself, i.e. commonly called personality. Psychism. Sensitivity. Domesticity.

MERCURY; Intellect. Evasive and quick. Communication. Organization. Logic. Learning.

VENUS; Love and the love life. Relationship with the group consciousness. Art. Sharing.

MARS; Strength. Vitality. Assertiveness. Lust to express. Activity. Desire to excel. The power which builds and destroys. Human animal drive.

JUPITER; Giving. Expansion. Link from Creation to Creator. Law of love. Justice. Law.

SATURN; Taskmaster. Dispenser of Karma. Time. Transformation. Contraction. Self-discipline.

The following three exterior planets affect the whose of mankind more than the individual man.

URANUS; Intuition. Innovative genius. Nonconforming. Higher consciousness.

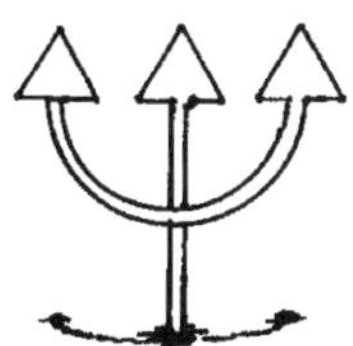

NEPTUNE; Mysticism. Dreaminess. General spirituality. Consciousness of universe instead of individuality.

PLUTO; Force of regeneration. That agent which causes the transformation mentioned above in Saturn. Redeemer. Uncovers that which is hidden. Channels power. The afterlife and that which goes on after termination.

These attributions are what the Winged Disk finds most suitable. Nothing is cast in stone, and slight variations may sometimes be considered valid. At this point keep an open mind, as the details of astrological debate are of little relevance.

The Four Quadrants

Little is generally known about the meaning of the four quadrants of the horoscope, nor has much been written about them. Here is how to interpret their meanings, so you can apply them to your own chart.

1st Quadrant: *Subjective Consciousness* (the "personal"): Starts on the first day of Aries (Vernal Equinox) to the last day of Gemini (Summer Solstice). Awareness of your native self as determined by your birth, and how your bring it out, as well as how you project and utilize it. Ego consciousness. Individuation.

2nd Quadrant: *Subjective Consciouness* (non-personal): Starts on the first day of Cancer (Summer Solstice) to the last day of Virgo (Autumnal Equinox). How you relate and integrate external things into your life, i.e., "group consciousness."

3rd Quadrant: *Objective Consciousness* (non-personal): Starts on the first day of Libra (Autumnal Equinox) to the last day of Sagitarius (Winter Solstice). Awareness of things and people "outside" of you and generally not related to you personally. How well your creativity will be expressed to others. In general, your awareness of others and their effects on you.

4th Quadrant: *Objective Consciousness:* Starts on the first day of Capricorn (Winter Solstice) to the first day of Aries (Vernal Equinox). Awareness of your social, business, political and spiritual power including spiritual identity and humanitarian growth of mankind. How you affect others and the "outside world".

The sign passing in the Ascendant (line separating Pisces from Aries) is symbolic of the awareness of the self. The sign passing over the cusp (line) separating Gemini from Cancer represents one's own consciousness. The sign passing over the cusp-line of Virgo to Libra is your awareness of the world relative to yourself. The cusp-line which separates Sagittarius from Capricorn represents consciousness and reaction to all that is external to yourself.

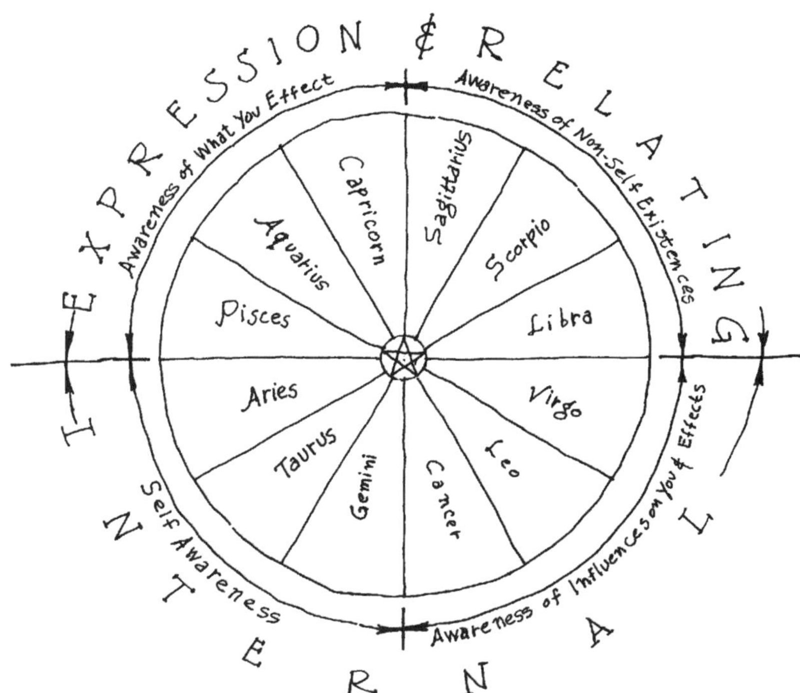

The quadrants explain the general flavor of the chart to be interpreted. Here we see the meaning of the quadrants that must be employed in a good interpretation.

96

Alchemical Teachings

"God (Kether) conforms itself into Father (Chokmah) and Mother (Binah) and thus begets a son."

According to this science, our system is neither matriarchal or patriarchal because the universe is neither. Alchemy deals with a mystical substance depicted in the Art card, which is a result of combining both positive and negative poles to create a third homogeneous "state". This concept was secretly borrowed and recorded in some traditions manifested as: the Keys of St. Peter, The Crook and Flail of Osiris, the double serpents or trunks of the Tree of Eden.

The writings of the alchemists can easily be understood by Adepts. The aspirant must be prudently taught of these matters; the art of alchemy is only taught to very advanced initiates of Magick. However, it is useful to have a concept of what is meant by this *summum bonum* (The Great Work).

All things and all life is comprised of a) a body of elements, b) and intelligible character and c) a true Identity (soul).

By transcending the body, the soul "flies" (liberates itself from restriction). The link between Kether and Malkuth is the most important one in the process. "Nouveau alchemy intellectuals" neglect the relevant link, propagating direct union with this God-level and minimizing inner perfection that makes you a fit receptacle that attracts the god force to you.

The alchemical axiom "As above, so below..." [1] is an important theme in Hermetic Magick. It tells the aspirant that he or she cannot cause change or attain on the spiritual plane without being able to cause change or attain on the physical as well. To neglect developing a divine attitude and power over manifestation keeps the aspirant regretfully from reaching the goal. Purity is true human nature, the execution of one's identity.

In order to perceive the Higher self, transcending the limita-

1. Hermes Trismegistus

tions of the intellect is essential. One cannot egotistically explain that which is infinite and beyond comprehension. The distorted idea that God made man in Its own image really means magickally, that It made man in Its own imagination—God, not base material. However, this Essence exists in all matter and energy. So it is not correct to say God did not create the base elements. But man, by his intellectual ego, perceived himself to be separated from spirit and by the fall from grace, and distilled into matter (i.e.essence, or self) as is explained next. The word God means pure unity, untainted by circumstance.

As you know from Qabalah (explained in Part II), force alone is male but is not God because "Its" potential to exist has still not culminated. So force,[2] which emanates from a perfected unity of All, has not yet transformed itself into what we call "God." In order for this force to be made manifest, form is required which is female and passive—the opposite of force.[3] It is only the combination of these two together that makes manifestation; thus this expression of force is made possible only through the faculty of form, the female. The Fool when

Art refers to the art of nature in which the Adept, by clarity, can seperate, perfect and recombine inferior manifestations which become "excellent."

2. Being only force or form is restriction. It is not complete
3. All force takes a form of its own. The force of electricity takes on the form of a lightning bolt; the force of gravity condenses matter, taking on the form of a planet, or descending cool air to take on the form of wind; the force of magnetism takes on the form of a compass needle pointing north.

distinct uses the pregnant virgin, the Empress, to produce a form, which is then called Jehovah, "I AM," and is beyond gender or element since they are results, i.e., "God's offspring." God divides Itself into equal and opposite poles (see Supernal Triangle, pg.57).

To reconcile light and darkness, fire and water, plus and minus, that-which-is and that-which-is-not is the object of alchemy both spiritual and laboratory; to bring matter back to spirit. Matter has become limited in manifestation, and although it emanates from God, it is not pure spirit. It is kept separate from spirit by certain influences known as the Qliphoth, whose job is to pull Creation away from Creator. The instinct of all matter is to revert back to spirit (its purest state), in which it existed before such influences. God, also known as Nature, has created this balance of polarity.

Thus polarity only exists on the physical plane. Unity only exists as nothingness or formlessness, before it divides itself into separate parts, each being incomplete. The act of Unity dividing itself into separate fragments is called the Creation. One of the fragments is physical manifestation (i.e. Malkuth). Thus Creator and its reflection (Creation) are opposite poles. If there was no separation, every star, every element would be perfect and therefore without a body and beyond the duality of life and death, because unity is the total presence of spirit and therefore the absence of manifestation or form. This state of perfection is called God, a unity that annihilates restriction. Aleister Crowley said that "every man and woman is a star," each whole within their true selves, complete and perfect by virtue of the fact that no two share the same unique orbit. Each has an individual Will, which when performed is the divine Will of God. Thus the solar system works unhampered with each universal body doing only its own Will.

The Principles

In alchemy we deal with principles. The principle of sulphur is activity and origination. It is attributed to the supernal (spiritual) triangle of Kether, Chokmah and Binah. The principle of salt symbolizes the opposite; rigidity, to corporeal appearance; reflection of the soul which forms the body. It symbolizes the Magickal triangle of Netzach, Hod, Yesod, where phenomena of Nature are observable and within the realm of man. Simple Magick (not attainment which should accompany Magick) belong there. The most important principle is mercury, the link which connects the higher and the lower. It is mutable and transforms the other principles back and forth. Mercury is attributed to the moral triangle of Chesed, Geburah and Tiphareth.

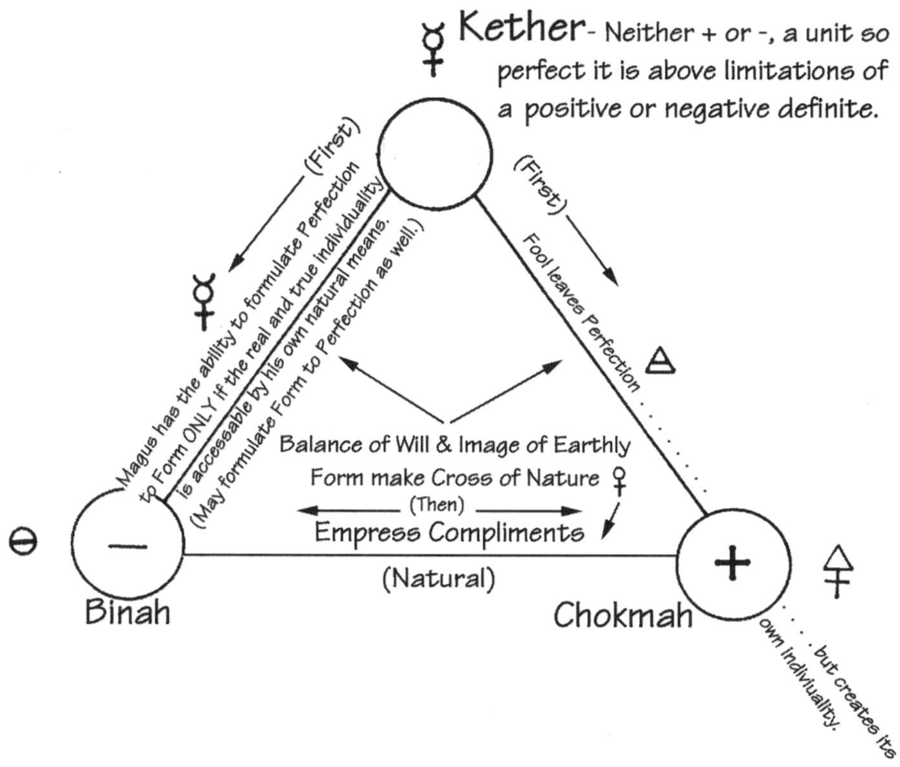

The author's diagram shows the complimentary parts of the alchemical sulpher which exists above the abyss and contains all duality coexisting undiminished.

To get to the essence of matter, life, and your soul, one must be cognizant of and master all of the principles which are methods of how the elements act. (For example, fire can act like sulphur, and have mercury or salt characteristics).

"What is the relationship of alchemy to one's spiritual growth?" By understanding Nature, you understand yourself.

Also, the adept, of course, does not cause physical change for entertainment or riches. It is an assertion of his Will over circumstance.

Are the popular uses of the word alchemy (mental alchemy, sexual alchemy, creative alchemy, etc.) valid? Only as comparative allegories. However, both laboratory alchemy and spiritual alchemy must be worked together. Do you know that metallurgists in Germany pray at the place of the athanor, the alchemical oven, before they begin their smelt? Why should not the crystal kingdom be so respected? Therefore, the end product of the alchemist is the actual spirit of the first matter. This condensate is the elixir of life that prolongs the Magickian's life, if taken daily, for a thousand or more years! First matter is not the matter that the Magickian deals with first, but last! It is viewed from the Creator's perspective. Every book protects such knowledge, leading the reader to believe the contrary.

When you are spiritually attained enough to cause such change, you are of great value to the spiritual development of the race. It is beneficial to The Great White Brotherhood that you stay around longer rather than having you and your knowledge terminate prematurely.

Those who have read *The Fulcanelli Phenomenon* know that one who has attained to such a degree must go underground and fabricate his death and adopt a new identity for obvious reasons. Thus, little is known of any man who has so attained. (How many "deaths" has the popular St. Germain had? And how many times have they been revealed as fraudulent? Further, how many medical men and others have been indicted for falsifying the documents of his death"?)

Remember, when reading alchemical literature that opposites must be combined and that the formula is to explain the method of becoming "King" (Kether). Successful union allows one to cross the abyss.

The practice of alchemy is the search for the soul. Plant alchemy is the first stage. The next is animal and the final is mineral. By perfecting metals we perfect man and plants at the same time. By perfecting man, we perfect only plants at the same time. Please contemplate this. This is necessary because all things of each kingdom grow simultaneously.

By the code of alchemy, we extract the mercury of the metal. This isolated substance reduces it to its first matter (Spirit). "Medicine" in alchemical literature really refers to "the elixir" which produces the stone that makes the lead to gold transformation. Don't take the words literally!

The Rebis is the united state of matter before the disruptive fall of man which seperated matter into male and female opposites.

The laboratory process takes a week. The preparation of your spirit takes a great deal longer!

In this simple and very preliminary concordance we must include other common codes and symbols you will run across in further study. First let us look at the all-important colors of the stone in the process. Although the transmutation goes through

102

the colors of the peacock's tail (thus was Notre Dame—the world's most profound and ancient alchemical laboratory worked by thousands of m agickal monks) there are three symbolic colors to describe the attainment of the process: Black = purification. The body reverts to its component parts that are purified and hence turn white. At that time they become perfect and realize their native goal (Will) and being mature turn red.

The Temple Of Man

An unhealthy Magickian cannot bring down healthy forces. The energies conducted take on the same character as the operator. Thus, in order to prevent any accidents, the Magickian must be pure not only of mind and emotion, but of body as well. By using the great laws of Nature, anyone can partake of the luxury of physical attainment.

It is an old but true axiom that the body is man's temple. *Man, Grand Symbol of the Mysteries* by M.P. Hall, is a very good treatise that explains this according to ancient tradition.

Avoid destructive foods: meat in particular.

It is essential for anyone who is going to cause change in his life to maintain a healthy life in *all* the four worlds. Bear in mind that your life cannot be what you want if any part is out of control, so the aspirant must control all aspects of your life.

Here are some basics the pursuer of The Art must consider:

Diet:
Avoid destructive foods: meat in particular. Sugar and salt are next most important to avoid. (Substitute honey if necessary and tamari for example.) You can eliminate these foods from your diet slowly, if need be. Drink water and fresh juices instead of caffeinated and carbonated drinks. Don't buy liquids in plastic containers. Avoid intoxication. If you smoke, quit now! Avoid anything that will artificially stimulate, depress, or otherwise alter your natural state. Take a vitamin supplement if necessary. However one can usually derive the proper vitamins from a well-balanced diet. Don't take megadoses of any

product! The Law of Nature is if a little is good, a lot is not always better! Only take vitamins derived from living, natural sources, never synthetic.

Read *all* food labels! Never eat a food if you don't know what you're eating! Beware of animal products hidden in food. You cannot avoid sugar or salt added to food, so abstain from adding such from the table. But this doesn't mean you should eat the junk foods that contain them!

Never eat "fortified" or "enriched" "foods." They slowly poison the body, mind, and spirit. They are substances to which certain laboratory-manufactured chemicals have been added to qualify them as "fit for human consumption." The problem is the additions are not from healthy sources.

Health food stores are expensive. If you cannot afford the luxury of organic foods that's alright. Shop wisely at the supermarket.

Most "healthy" foods don't contain destructive ingredients but read labels and pass up foods that do.

Stay away also from milk, white flour, and oils that are not cold pressed, I.E., hydrogenated. They are dangerous.

Eat creatively. If you don't know how to cook or are afraid to try new dishes...experiment simply...learn. Buy both *Diet For a Small Planet* and *Recipes for a Small Planet*. There are many good vegetarian cookbooks available (Molly Katzen's are among the best) and practically every restaurant can accommodate the vegetarian. Just ask!

Moderation is the main ingredient!

Keep a well stocked cabinet of simple versatile basics for all times. Exotic, hard-to-find ingredients are usually discouraging unless you enjoy the pursuit of them!

Don't drink water a half an hour before and two to four hours after a meal (and never during a meal).

Variety is the key to a good diet.

Refer to a "food combining" book for the proper and improper food combinations. Basically eat natural sugars such as fruits and other carbohydrates first, proteins last.

If there's no peace and time to eat, skip it!

Body:
Don't wear tight clothes or clothes that "just feel un-

comfortable."

Maintain a healthy weight! For an approximation of what you should weigh, use trial and error, only if you're impeccably honest. Otherwise look at a weight chart. Then deduct 10% from the indicated weight, which is always based on a fat American.

Diet when you are ready. Don't try it otherwise; you'll only fail. Resign yourself to the fact that being overweight is uncomfortable, dangerous, causes premature, degenerative illness and shortens life span.

> *Don't role model after people. Do your Will.*

Exercise safely. Do it regularly. Everyone can do some sort of exercise. Stagnation causes problems.

Remember the principle that no man or woman should neglect: weight, diet, exercise, abuse, etc. are usually accumulative. As example, three pounds gained in one year, can add up to 30 pounds in ten years. So at age forty, you can build your tomb by the age of 50.

Don't role model after people. Do your Will.

Building The Temple

Know your herbs. Get a couple of good herb books such as John Lust's *The Herb Book*.

Allopathic medicine is often bad. But, occasionally, if necessary it must be taken! However, don't fall into the "pill" society. Once you establish a good state of health, medicine will not be necessary.

Is it too late? If you start now, spending two to five years insuring a happy, vital, and healthy life-style, you'll be accustomed to and well enough to avoid all of the usual "problems" your friends and family have.

There's no need for fanaticism. Health experts often don't agree because not everything is known about good health. So, when reading, let intuition be your guide.

Why Vegetarianism?

It is not the intention here to attempt to persuade readers to become vegetarians. Instead, this is an objective answer to those who want to know the advantages of vegetarianism.

A vegetarian is one who eats no animal products. Some people call themselves vegetarians but still eat fish and chicken; be assured those two species still belong to the animal kingdom—they have flesh and blood just like a cow or a human or a deer. Also he or she uses a minimum of leather, only where necessary.

There are three issues to consider in regard to vegetarianism. They are: nutritional, spiritual, and moral.

Nutritionally, the alkaline-based digestive system of humans will not properly break down substantial acid substances, the greatest of which is meat. (Also, the amount of cholesterol in meat is unhealthy.)

Colon cancer is rampant! This is caused by the slow evacuation and the putrefaction in the colon of the remains of meat. Lifelong vegetarians never suffer from such an illness.

The type and amount of oils in meat are unhealthy and they turn rancid upon the death of the animal. The flesh and blood also began to putrify as soon as the animal is killed.

Many meat eaters believe that meat is the sole source of protein. However, the quality of this protein is so poor that little of it can ever be utilized by humans because it is incomplete and lacks the correct combination of amino acids, the building blocks of protein.

Studies show that the average American gets five times the amount of protein needed. It is a common medical fact that excess protein is dangerous, the prime danger being that uric acid (the waste product produced in the process of digesting protein) attacks the kidneys, breaking down the kidney cells called nephrons. This condition is called nephritis; the prime cause of it is overburdening the kidneys.

More usable protein is found in one tablespoon of tofu or soybeans than the average serving of meat!

Have you ever seen what happens to a piece of meat that stays in the sun for three days? Meat can stay in the warmth of the intestine for at least four days until it is digested. It does nohting but wait for passage. Often, it usually stays there for much longer, traces remaining for up to several months. Colonic therapists always see meat passing through in people who have been vegetarians for several years, thus indicating that meat remains undigested there for a long time. Occasionally this has been documented in twenty year vegetarians!

The environmental conditions of the intestine are perfect for an enormous array of organisms to breed. Note also that the "friendly" bacteria normally found in the intestines are not powerful enough to attack the meat substance since it is not their purpose—instead the opposite occurs. Some organisms that breed on the decaying animal substance also attack those intestinal bacterials.

> *Many meat eaters believe that meat is the sole source of protein.*

Some vegetarians claim they are more satisfied after they eat. The reason for this is that there are fewer ketones (protein-digestive substances) formed when vegetable protein is digested. To many ketones cause a trace amount of nausea which one normally interprets as a decreased desire for food due to this uncomfortable and slight degree of queasiness. Although the body calls for more food, the taste buds tolerate less. This is the danger of the popular high-protein diet substances on the market. This abnormally high level of ketones is called ketosis and refers to the state of starvation that the body incurs due to the inability of the appetite to call for nutrition. The high amount of complex carbohydrates required to overthrow this condition is never recognized by most Americans who eat the wrong type of carbohydrates. Also, when the blood ketone level is too high, it results in abnormally acidic blood, called acidosis.

Tigers or lions who eat meat and grow strong on it have acid-based digestive systems. Also, their intestines are in a straight run of about five feet long, not twisted and turned, layer over layer, compacted into a small area like the human intestine, which is twenty feet long.

Frequently when certain animal carcasses are found to have cancerous growths in the butchering and trimming process, they are simply carved out by the butcher before it hits the market. How safe is this for human consumption?

Everybody knows about the hormones and other substances which are fed to animals. But did you know that in some places they also feed the large animals concrete to add weight and saleability?

Some farmers have started to implement a new system (still in its infancy and hopefully a doomed one) in which they feed the larger animals their own freeze-dried, unsterilized feces. Just imagine the money that could be saved on costly feed!

Did you also know that up until recently one-third of all chickens were leukemic and were still allowed to be sold? Today, however, powerful chemicals are fed daily to the chickens to attempt to control chicken leukemia. As a matter of fact, since as far back as 1950, arsenic has been the standard chemical given to poultry within the entire industry. A farmer just cannot afford not to use arsenic! So the chicken eater consumes this arsenic legally...and it accumulates without ever being expelled!

Poultry is often frozen for up to two years. Cold temperatures do not kill all species of bacteria. Worse than this, as it is shipped and stored, most frozen meat is thawed and refrozen many times. This is almost unavoidable.

> *Poultry is often frozen for up to two years.*

Meat eaters suffer more frequently from various types of food poisoning than non-meat eaters—so much so that statistics show that every American has had food poisoning on at least one occasion. When you've felt ill, out-of-sorts, had diarrhea, or were just a little sick to your stomach, no doubt you had not the slightest idea that you had been poisoned by scavengers living off the dead carcass you just ate.

Next there is the subject of fish. Fish do not have a waste system to expel or handle toxins, and any fish that inhabits the waters near where fisheries do their fishing, especially in the Eastern part of the country, are swimming in polluted waters.

When you eat fish, you're eating toxins. The FDA only examines 20% of all fish being sold.

There are said to be one hundred irradiation facilities being set up commercially around the country. Some are already commencing their operation. All sausages and many fruits and vegetables are now being irradiated. The scientific research on its effects is inconclusive and it will take several years until its dangers are recognized and it can be legislated out of the food industry. The purpose of irradiation is to destroy the odor of bacterial action on meat when it turns bad; thus you will no longer be able to smell a piece of meat to see if it has putrefied! Irradiation is legal and the government has recently turned down a bill that would require a visible symbol on the package indicating to the consumer that the food has been irradiated. This means meat will stay on the shelves (according to the industry) five times longer than it does now.

The reason this new process was invented is because there is so much nuclear waste that there is nothing else to do with it! So the nuclear industry came up with this "useful" suggestion of selling their discard to the food industry (a repeat of t he aluminum industries scheme with its waste product fluoride).

Meat is costly and it is the most wasteful source of resources. When one removes meat from his or her diet, a whole new world of eating opens up. Cooking and preparing vegetarian style is no more time consuming than cooking meat. It costs less than half as much to eat vegetarian as it does to eat meat. There are excellent, nutritious, and easy to prepare vegetarian dishes that are Italian, Chinese, Indian, Mideastern, French, Spanish, etc.

Additionally, one can enjoy many other foods that he has never tasted because of the meat rut. Most consumers have eaten no more than five or six varieties of beans and legumes—less than 10% of what is available and grains, including different appetizing types of wheat, nuts, and seeds. And they can be prepared very creatively!

Other peas, lentils, vegetables, and cereals, commonly found in every grocery or delicatessen, are usually neglected. These can provide exciting alternatives to the usual meats. The rules for cooking these are always the same, but the individual touch comes in their use and preparation. So learning to cook one new food item means you understand how to cook all the other food items in that category.

The spiritually aspiring person attempts to work on his- or herself. The purpose of spiritual growth is to move away from the animal nature into the more human nature that God intended for us to have. Meat eating inhibits this. Again, the same science—that sometimes attempts to ignore the existence of a force higher than man—also has proved, in the laboratory, that aggression levels are much higher in meat eaters than nonmeat eaters! The animal instincts become more powerful every time you eat meat.

When animals are slaughtered, fear and aggression enzymes are shot into their cells from their glands and other organs, just as in humans, and are part of the dead carcass that goes on to the food store. They remain in the meat until the consumer ingests those same enzymes, which are molecularly very similar to those found in humans.

Most spiritual people believe in the aura. Kirilian photography shows us that a force field remains around dead or amputated tissue. You adopt that animal aura when you eat a dead animal. Is it not personal evolution that the spiritual aspirant is interested in? If so, meat eating is urgently prohibited.

Meat is the most inefficient form of food to produce. One fact for those who are not familiar with the waste required to produce meat: It takes 10,000 gallons of water to produce one pound of steak (for feed, washing, etc.). That could pose quite a threat to the dwindling and endangered water supplies.

The moral aspect goes along with the spiritual one, in which one must question the necessity and the method as well as the karma of killing animals. However, everyone has their own mores which they must determine for themselves. It is not the purpose of this book to force a specific moral behavior on anyone.

Note: In California, cows are using as much water as humans! Gary Null, in his book *Cleaner, Better, Simpler*, documented that pasture is being irrigated in near-desert conditions simply to raise beef! In one year they used 5.3 million acre-feet, which is as much as all the citizens used, including drinking, bathing, watering lawns, and swimming pools!

Water is becoming a valuable commodity in the world (as

prophesied). Daily, this once-abundant fluid is becoming more precious. The water economy of raising cows, compared to raising vegetables, is ridiculously impractical.

Natures Medicine Chest

<u>(The substances and information herein mentioned are for historical or curiosity purposes only, and although some persons may use them for the purpose of maintaining good health they should not be substituted for proper medical advice in the treatment of illness or injury. In such cases a medical physician should be consulted.)</u>

To unite with Nature, God, (or whatever your nomenclature for Diety) and to comprehend Divine Universal Phenomena, one must experience all Its facets. So, the Hermetic Magickian studies of herbology.

Every plant has a similar vibration to a particular planet. Every part of the body also vibrates to the same frequency as a certain planet.

Now, since what occurs on a more subtle plane makes itself shown on this material plane, by looking at the characteristics of a plant we can determine its true Nature. This practice requires a deep psychic sense that is objective, i.e., above prejudice and preconceived intellectual subjective notions.

Paracelsus, the alchemical philosopher, had this kind of vision and he brought forth from this phenomenon the phrase "the doctrine of signatures."

One example of the higher plane representing itself in the lower is the herb eyebright. It looks like bright eyes! Wild pansies have heart-shaped leaves and are excellent cardiac tonics. It is also said that local plants cure local people, since they are subject to the same vibrations and environment. The willow tree, which grows in dampness, is said to be used for rheumatism which is aggravated by dampness. Those who have cultivated their inner vision will see the doctrine of signatures in many plants.

Herein are given the many uses for herbs on the physical

level, but remember that the four worlds are related—none are distinct.

Herbs work by providing the particular category of life force to the user. You can feel the living activity of the herbs as you become sensitive.

Because of their pleasantness, affordability, gentleness and efficacy, herbs are easily utilized. They may be made into tests, capsules, tinctures, oils, or even applied topically.

How To Make A Herbal Tea (Infusion)

In general, for leaves or cut and sifted herbs, simply pour boiling water over the herb. If desired, put the herbs in an infuser. Steep, covered for about thirty minutes, or until room temperature. Strain the herbs out (save them for your garden compost!) or leave them in, it makes no difference. Herbal teas are meant to be sipped slowly. Usual dosages are two to four cups per day. Adjust to suit the needs. Continue using herbs one to two weeks after symptoms cease to avoid recurrence. Herbs work gently and slowly.

The only other thing you must know about teas is that roots are stronger and must be brought to a boil, and then kept covered at a simmer for up to thirty minutes until they can be used.

Powdered herbs can be taken as follows: Put a sixth (approx) of a teaspoon of the powder on a tissue or starch paper, and roll it up. This "capsule" is then swallowed. Take three to four capsules three to four times per day. Plant cellulose capsules are now available at most health food stores. Gelatin capsules should be avoided as they are made from animal fat. A tea is as effective as a capsule. A lot of people don't take herbs on an empty stomach.

To make a fomentation, make a strong tea, take a clean white cloth and soak it in the tea, then apply the cloth to the affected area (make sure the liquid is not too hot). Leave on area until the cloth becomes cool. Repeat as necessary.

Again, and in addition to the legal disclaimer above, we state that the following formulae are reports of uses and causes, and merely in the interest of providing a whole spectrum of information and curiosity, for a literary purposes only.

The Formulae

ADDICTION: 1/2 part Siberian Ginseng, 1 part Skullcap, combined in 3 caps, 3-5 x per day.

ALLERGY: Eyebright.

APHRODISIAC: Siberian Ginseng, Damiana.

ASSIMILATION: Goldenseal (lowers blood sugar), Cayenne

ASTHMA: Wood Betony, Burdock, Comfrey or Ephedra (Ma Huang).

BROKEN BONES: Comfrey root.

CARBUNCLES: Burdock root tea.

CHOLESTEROL: Cayenne, Panax Ginseng (lowers blood sugar).

CIRCULATION: Butcher's Broom, Rosemary Oil and Cayenne combined in 1 cap, 3 x per day.

CONGESTION: Goldenseal and Myrrh snuff for nasal or pulmonary. Comfrey root for lungs. Also, Licorice Root and Bay-berry. For pulmonary congestion, Lobelia fomentation on chest.

CONSTIPATION: Cinnamon, Cloves, or Ginger root to prevent gripping. Also, 2 cups water in A.M., exercise, wheat germ and garlic.

COUGH: Elecampane, Slippery Elm as an expectorant, and diuretic.

DIABETES: Pau D'arco 3-6 caps per day. 1 cup tea 4-6 x per day.

DIARRHEA: Nettle. Raspberry leaves (good for infants) 1 oz. infused in 2 cups water, 2 x per day.

EXPECTORANT: Comfrey root capsule or poultice. Elecampane good for mucous dripping into lungs. Tiger balm.

EYE WASH: 1 tsp Goldenseal root and 1 tsp Boric acid to 1 pint of hot water. Then dilute 1 tsp of this with 1/2 cup of water.

FEVER: Peppermint. If over 102 degrees (adults) if sick:

Yarrow & Elder flowers. If healthy: Elder flowers and Skull-cap. No cold drinks during treatment.

FLU: Ginger, Cayenne, Goldenseal, Licorice, or Bayberry and Peppermint (as diaphoretic), or Peppermint and Elder Flowers.

GAS: Peppermint.

GASTRIC JUICES: To secret and increase bile flow use Goldenseal 1-2 caps 3-4 x a day. 1 glass with meals.

HAY FEVER: Eyebright 1 tsp. infused, 1-2 cups per day.

HEADACHE: Peppermint oil applied to temples. Peppermint tea, Blessed Thistle (toxin headaches), Wood Betony

HEART: Panax Ginseng (produces testosterone), Blessed Thistle, Peppermint (for strength)

HEMORRHOIDS: Burdock tea on a wash cloth. Fast, drink water and carrot juice (in equal parts). Use vitamin B as a suppository. Use Comfrey root poultice and drinks much Red Raspberry tea.

HERPES: Burdock root and Echinacea Angustifolia tea, internal and external.

HIGH BLOOD PRESSURE: Garlic, Barberry root 1/2 tsp. with water (boiled briefly) 1/2-1 cup per day. Siberian Ginseng 1-3 caps, 2-3 x per day.

INFECTION: Goldenseal and Myrrh. 1/4 tsp. ea. in 1/2 cup water.

KIDNEY: Diuretics: Uva Ursi, 1 cup 3-4 x per day, 3 caps 3 x per day. Goldenseal, 1 cap 3 x per day. To clean uric acid use Burdock Root tea.

MEMORY: Blessed Thistle.

MENSTRUATION: Cramps (to moderate): Red Raspberry (can decrease flow) Excessive flow-Nettle. Blessed Thistle, 1 tsp. per cup, 2-3 x per day. Insufficient flow - Red Raspberry. (After miscarriage use emmenagogues).

NERVINES: Vitamin B andC, Valerian (accumulates in the liver) Skullcap.

PMS: Check potassium level; water, exercise, Parsley. If cramps, 2 parts calcium, 1 part magnesium. If no cramps, 2 pt. magnesium, 1 pt. calcium.

POISON IVY: Strong Sassafras tea applied with cotton.

POLYPS: Bayberry bark applied to polyps.

PYORRHEA: Goldenseal and Myrrh.

SHINGLES: Use an alternative, the best of which is Echinacea Angustfolia.
SICK ROOMS: Fumigate with Juniper berries.
SINUS: Stuffed: 5-10 drops of water. Drink 1-2 quarts of water. Infection; Goldenseal and Myrrh, 1/4 tsp. each in 1/2 cup water, wait 10 minutes, add 1/2 cup water, pour in nose. Mucous only: 1 part Bayberry Bark, 2 part Goldenseal, snuff.
SKIN: Vitamin A.
SKIN CANCER: Red Clover blossom.
SORE THROAT: Echinacea Angustifolia 2-3 caps, 3-6 x per day or 4-6 cups tea per day. Gargle with strong Red Clover blossom tea or Red Raspberry tea. Chew Slippery Elm.
STYES: see Carbuncles.
SWOLLEN GLANDS: same as sore throat but every two hours until swelling decreases. Also fast with fruit or vegetable juices. Enemas and high colonics.
TOOTHACHE: Clove oil
TOXINS: To expel use a combination of Red Clover blossom, Dandelion Root, and Sassafras (the latter, if not anemic).
TRICK: Sassafras tea (be careful), add Goldenseal and White Oak bark. Douche.
ULCERS: Pau D'arco, Slippery Elm
U.T.I.: Nettle. Uva Ursi, 1 cup 3-4 x per day or 3 caps 3 x per day. Goldenseal, 1 cap 4 x per day.
VARICOSE VEINS: Wood Betony.
YEAST: Pau D'arco, 3 caps 3 x per day; acidophilus, 3 caps 3 x per day.

Consult *The Herb Book* by John Lust for further information.

Keeping Healthy In Winter

Because the weather takes its toll on your skin use a good emollient or lotion. Sweet almond oil (although fragrant) is effective. Also use a good hair conditioner.

To keep the feet warm in the winter, sprinkle a little cayenne in the shoes.

A good warming herb can keep you warm in the winter. Contrary to popular belief, Alcohol will drop the body temperature in the winter.

If the throat gets sore, chew on some Slippery Elm. It will provide relief immediately.

For sinus congestion, a combination of Goldenseal and Myrrh as a snuff can be effective.

If you expect to get sick because it is being subliminally suggested to you by others, or the media, you will cause it to manifest. Instead program yourself to refuse all sickness. The Magickian can have great control over his body!

10 Ways To Prevent Colds And Flu

1) Vitamin C should be obtained preferably by food, otherwise supplement 500 to 1000 mg. per day but never more than 250 mg. per dose.

2) Retaining body heat is important. The highest proportion of heat is lost through the head. Wear a hat. Dressing in layers is a more efficient heat-saving device than one single garment.

3) Keep the lungs clean through breathing exercises. Breathe deeply when in confined spaces. This will allow pulmonary air circulation to expel invading organisms. When someone in the home is sick, spray a mist of Juniper Berry tea or oil in the air to kill contagious bacteria.

4) Simple colds are usually transmitted through the eye tissues. Therefore keep your hands from touching them.

5) The immune system can ward off these illnesses if it is strong. Drink three cups of Pau D'arco herb tea or take three capsules three to four times per day. This is said to keep the immune system strong and healthy.

6) Going out on a cold day with open pores from bathing or damp hair will assuredly weaken your resistance.

7) Vitamin A (found in apples and carrots) can prevent infection.

8) Regular exercise will keep the organs from becoming weak and susceptible to infection.

9) Besides taking the proper vitamins and minerals in the diet, one should eat and drink cleansing and eliminative foods. Grains, green leafy vegetables, and various juices can facilitate cleansing. Also, foods high in niacin will keep blood capillaries from developing sludge and other such deposits.

10) If your heating system dries out your mucous membranes, put a pan of water on the radiator. The less stress on the lungs the better.

How To Lose Weight Using Herbs

KOLA NUTS: Kola nuts are a stimulant, containing natural constituents that are similar to the dangerous substitutes like caffeine or sugar which deplete, rather than fortify the body while increasing the metabolic process.

LICORICE ROOT: A favorite of herbalists, this can either be made into a tea or chewed in its raw stick form. Not only is it reported to assist in throat irritations, but it is said to cleanse the body of fat. By stimulating the liver, which processes fat, it increases its excretory functions. It also helps to eliminate fat stored in the body, it is an excellent substitute for sweets also! It can have a slight cleansing action on the blood. Because of its sweetness it diminishes the appetite slightly. It is not recommended for people with high blood pressure.

SARSAPARILLA: Its inherent hormonelike constituents stimulate the glands that purge the body of fatty poisons.

FENNEL: It soothes and tones the stomach, making it extremely efficient during a diet, expelling excess fluids and attacking excess fatty deposits.

BLADDERWRACK: High in iodine, it deteriorates cellulite accumulations, and by virtue of its natural occurrence in a plant, it does so more effectively, and is safer than iodine supplements.

HAWTHORN BERRIES: They aid in burning off fat. They also expel excess cholesterol deposits from the blood.

CHICKWEED: This is a natural diuretic. It also depresses the appetite.

CAPSICUM (Cayenne): Never heat this herb in cooking. The chemical change makes it irritating. When using it, add it to the pot after cooking and before serving. Don't use it if you have ulcers, though some authorities disagree. It increases circulation. An entire book could be written about the uses of this herb and still be incomplete. The increased circulation helps to expel fat and regulate cholesterol. Used in its dried but uncooked form, it can provide a valuable asset to the healthy dieter and health-oriented person.

BURDOCK ROOT: This is an excellent herb that flushes the accumulated toxins and wastes from the body. Thus, the efficiently operating system will burn off fat better. Just as Echinacea Angustofolia is probably the best known blood purifier, Burdock root is one of the best known body purifiers.

RASPBERRY LEAF: At the moment of food craving, drink a cup of this tea and the craving will more than likely disappear. It strengthens the metabolism and neurologically transmitted food signals are satisfied.

PARSLEY: This pleasant herb regulates the thyroid gland (the governor of the metabolic rate), which determines how much fat to burn and programs the appetite.

FENUGREEK: It works on the pituitary gland and regulates the appetite amazingly well. It is particularly effective in cravings for fatty foods.

RED CLOVER: It is usually recommended to replace that morning coffee boost and it does not have the caffeine crash let-down. It controls the appetite when it becomes a mental craving rather than a true need of the body for energy.

The Uses Of Peppermint Oil

It has been said that Nature has made her medicine cabinet in peppermint oil. The vibrations attributed to it are only in the essential oil, not in the fragrant oil.

It has been used for asthma, bronchitis, colds, dermatitis, diarrhea, fainting, fevers, flatulence, gallstones, headaches, hysteria, influenzae, mental fatigue, migraine, nausea, nervous disorders, palpitations, paralysis, ringworm, scabies, shock, toothache, and vomiting.

It is a pain reliever that can reduce inflammation, destroy bacteria, relieve spasms or cramps, reduce unnatural discharges, expel gas, fortify the brain tissue, provide an unobstructed flow of bile into the intestines, soothe by stimulation, promote late or scanty menstrual flow, expel lung congestion, reduce fever, stimulate the function of the liver and gallbladder, relieve nervous disorders, relieve gastric disorders, induce sweating, and raise the blood pressure.

For colds, flu, and minor respiratory problems, rub the oil on the chest, back, and affected area.

For muscular problems rub deep into the affected area. Apply directly on areas of pain or areas that require healing such as burns, warts, insect bites., For earaches rub it around the ear and put cotton in the ear. For headaches apply to the pulse points (where you feel the pulse in the head and neck area.)

For fainting, weakness, dizziness, motion sickness, or fatigue, apply to the forehead, neck, temples, and behind the ears.

Take internally for stomach ache, diarrhea, flu, etc. Put three to eight drops in a glass of water at room temperature.

For sore throats, use about three drops in the mouth. Also apply externally to the throat.

It can be applied to the teeth, gums or mouth and used with water as a gargle.

Occult Property Of Herbs

Besides their medicinal virtues, plants also have mystical or occult properties. Some people access these properties by burning herbs. Usually it is only necessary to carry them to be effective. One can also wear the oils, but this may not always be practical. No matter how plants are used for Magickal purposes, their attribution must be correct.

Just as every color has its own energy, so does every herb. By knowing your Qabalistic attributions, you will know how to apply the herbal and planetary knowledge.

To cleanse a person or home: An incense consisting of nutmeg, gum mastic, myrtle, and camphor is extremely good.

For clear or prophetic dreams: Use a lunar incense such as sandlalwood.

For health: Use a solar incense such as frankincense.

A general temple incense: Frankincense, lavender and myrrh will bring a nice vibration to the place of Magickal working.

Dream pillow (for sound and peaceful rest): The usual recipe

consists of marjoram, hops, and mugwort.
Agrimony: Cheerfulness.
Ambergris: Boldness.
Bayleaves: Pleasant dreams; also used for psychic protection.
Dragon's Blood: Protects people from negative entities.
Garlic: Repels evil.
Gum Mastic: Anything solar; also attributed to the Hierophant card.
Juniper: Protects people from negative entities, although not as potent or reliable as dragon's blood.
Lavender: Calmness.
Mandrake: Past life recall; astral projection; could be fatal if taken in any form internally.
Mint: Good for business abilities.
Patchouli: Causes things to manifest, sometimes good, sometimes evil.
Red Rose: Passion.
Saffron: Cultivates the mind.
Sage: Cleansing, said to repel negative entities.
Sandalwood: Very relaxing and rejuvenating, but it can be too mellow and induce melancholia with some people.

As attainment occurs, one understands that he or she is not his or her body. The soul (identity) is eternal. The body of elements dies. Often the two are confused for each other. This philosophy is taught here. Etching by Wm. Blake early 1800's.

The Soul

Spiritual growth culminating in unity with God is the will of every soul. An infant left alone in a house will crawl around until the entire house has been explored. It is human nature to expand and grow to fulfillment, leading finally to perfection, from incarnate necessity until transcendence of this has been performed. Ultimately when man's growth has been competed, the soul no longer needs the physical body. This is absolute happiness; perfection. It has been called nirvana, heaven, enlightenment, attainment, etc.

Simplified, the soul can be termed the perfection of the "true" person or Self. It is composed of many parts, except the physical body, which it does use. The soul never dies.

A Qabalistic explanation of the parts of the soul is an important part of the teachings of our magickal path. It may be difficult to understand for those who are not

> *Simplified, the soul can be termed the perfection of the "true" person or Self.*

working with the magickal arts. However, like all magickal study and practice, the aspirant will not realize its profundity until he is ready; when he himself is profound.

A Qabalistic Explanation Of The Parts Of The Soul

1. Neschamah

The first part of the human state is called the Neschamah. It corresponds to the Atziluth and the Briah (see page 59). It can be likened to the essential God-part of th individual. It is where consciousness and true identity meet. Above the abyss, the

Neschamah is part of those supernal forces that defy mortal description, but suffice it to say that where God dwells we cannot comprehend.[1] The Neschamah is the soul's inherent individuality, the pure character of the spirit. It is the "contact point" that is connected to (and the direct reflection of the) God-perfection-Total Unity without aberration.

1 (a). YECHIDAH

Within the Neschamah are two subclassifications. The Yeschidah, or Perfected Self, is first. It resides in Kether and is without limit. All twenty-two trumps are herein attributed. It is called the seed—the first "spark" of spirit, the first appearance of God. It is God in the soul.

1 (b). CHIAH

The second category of the Neschamah is the Chiah. It has a lower vibration and is described as the "fingerprint" or individuality. It is attributed to Chokmah and it is the character of the energy of the soul and contains primal vitality. The Aeon card (from the Thoth deck used by the Winged Disk, also may be the "Judgement" card in other decks) can be contemplated on for more information on this. Here the absolute individuality is defined: It is the finite aspect of the Yechidah, from which comes the identity that belongs exclusively to each individual soul...the essence of the true personality. Knowing it is called wisdom. To know a person's name in early Egyptian lore was to know his soul! It is how God reflects itself in a person.

The Neschamah resides in Binah[2] in form and may be studied there. It is how the soul is divinely meant to express its Chiah. In Binah, which is attributed to ego, we can see Neschamah as the Garden of Eden (intellect before it is given the knowledge of good or evil). The Neschamah precludes reasoning, and all the soul's "intuition" comes from it. Contemplate the Hanged Man card to learn more about this part.

---

1. The Sephir Yetzirah claims that one cannot see the face of God and live. This is not out of punishment, but because one who is attained enough to behold the Creative Force of the Universe is no longer restricted or subject to the laws of the body; to have such would hinder and restrict him from this attainment. Such would be similar to the Einsteinian spiritual-scientific revelation that as a body accelerates, it gains in mass and weight and slows down, so it can never reach the velocity of light.
2. Binah is always the consolidation of the supernal triangle. Thus practicing Magickians do operations directed at Binah, not Chokmah or Kether.

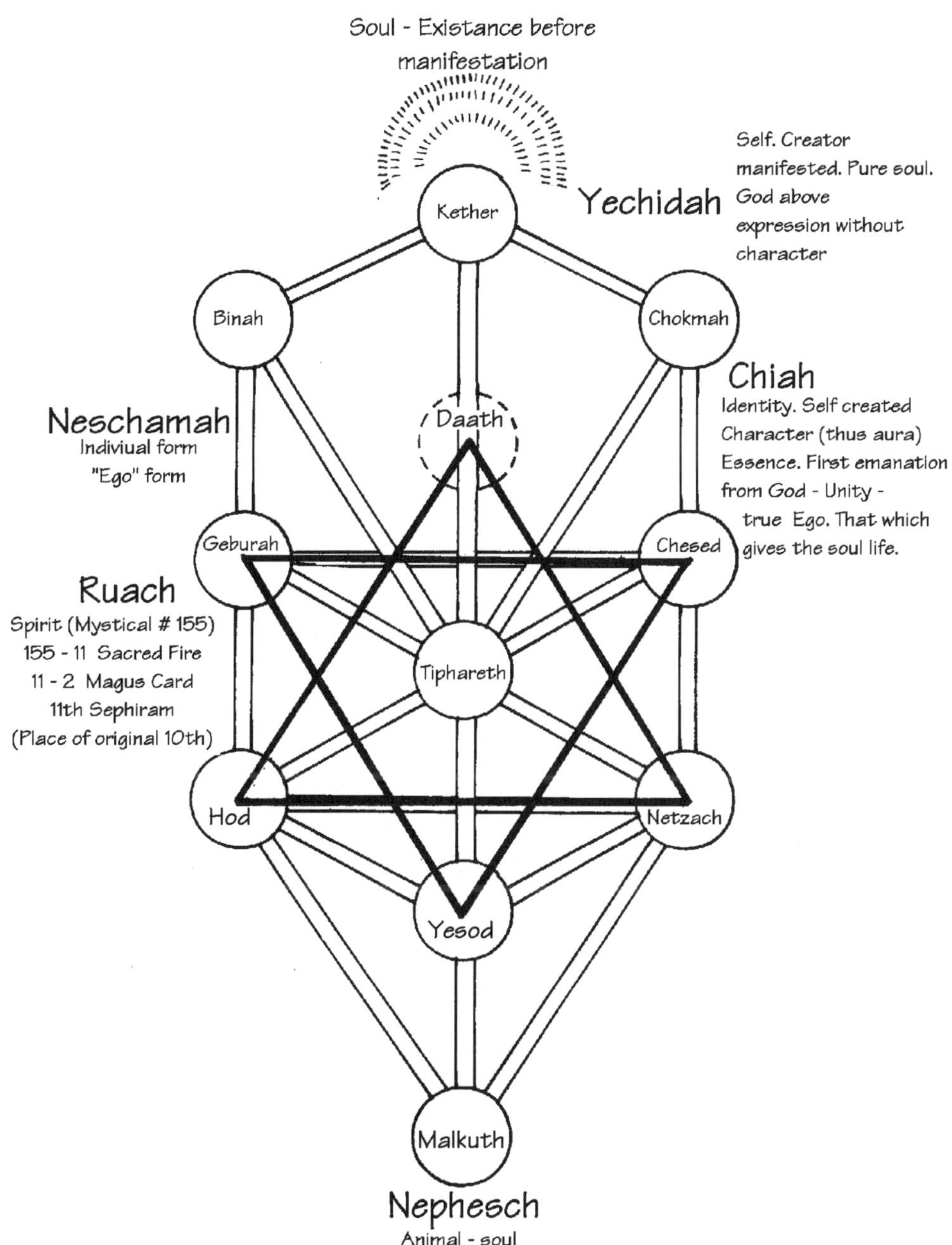
Soul - Existance before manifestation
Kether
Yechidah
Self. Creator manifested. Pure soul. God above expression without character
Binah
Chokmah
Chiah
Identity. Self created Character (thus aura) Essence. First emanation from God - Unity - true Ego. That which gives the soul life.
Daath
Neschamah
Indiviual form
"Ego" form
Geburah
Chesed
Ruach
Spirit (Mystical # 155)
155 - 11 Sacred Fire
11 - 2 Magus Card
11th Sephiram
(Place of original 10th)
Tiphareth
Hod
Netzach
Yesod
Malkuth
Nephesch
Animal - soul

2. RUACH

The second part of the soul is called the Ruach, reasoning. It is the link between the higher and the lower parts of the soul because it unites the two. The Ruach possesses the knowledge of good and evil. As reasoning, it is assigned to the Yetzirah. Studying the Fool card will reveal more about this part of the soul. It can be called the Spirit.

Both the Neschamah and the Ruach are the parts of the mind. The Neschamah is the higher part; the Ruach the rational intellect or lower part.

3. NEPHESH

The third part of the soul is the Nephesh (or animal instincts). It is also called the animal soul because it is mere stimulus and response. It is attributed to the Assiah and sees, feels, and provides the physical force and appetites that occur on this physical plane. Because the Nephesh caters to fulfilling only the basic requirements of man as an animal species, it can keep the higher soul from evolving if it is allowed to dominate. It does provide bodily function i.e. heartbeat, respiration, etc, to keep the body satisfied. Study the Empress card for further revelations.[3]

It is important to know that the Nephesh is the opposite, but compliment to the Neschamah. It can be counterproductive partly because of its attachment to lifeless elements. Alchemically, the Nephesh is referred to as the dragon. The Zohar says that the hexagram is the Nephesh united with the Neschamah in harmony and dedicated towards the fulfillment of the individual soul (life purpose).

The descent of spirit into matter is divine; it should not be regarded as unholy. After all, the Qabalist says that Kether is in Malkuth and Malkuth is in Kether. In Genesis it states "The Lord God breathed into his nostrils the breath of life and man became a living soul."[4] This is the Nephesh. Never think that there is no spirit in matter, for the seed of spirit is found there.

These are the parts of the soul as explained from a Qabalistic vantage point. The keyes of Alchemy are also Qabalistic and a

---

3. The conversion of matter to spirit in alchemy is focalized in the Assiah. Some authorities differ as to whether the Assiah can be attributed to Malkuth only, or Malkuth and Yesod. Both views are valid.

4. Genesis 2:7

few should be studied in this chapter to make it complete.

Fire and water, though opposites, are "children" of one substance. The third principle is attributed to earth, the material basis. In some alchemical stories an important concept regarding a certain union is described: it can be likened to the Ruach uniting with the Neschamah, whereas the Ruach becomes perfected to return to its natural place and unite to the Nephesh. In this way the Nephesh becomes perfected as well! Each part remains in its specific function but perfectly so, for the fulfillment of the entire soul (Will).

Thus, in spiritual Alchemy, it is important to establish the connecting link between the two polarities, otherwise the perfected energy cannot flow. It is further explained that Spirit acts through the Nephesh. The cause needs to be treated in this spagyric art, not the symptom. Fix the Ruach to assist in the purification of the Nephesh. Achieving this, the Neschamah can be free to flow properly through the Ruach onto the Nephesh. But remember that the Ruach can only be purified by the Neschamah! Thus, the union of the higher to the lower depends on Ruach as the intermediary. This is the glory of the goal.

The next section will be briefly touch upon other Qabalistic correspondences to the parts of the soul, namely their correlation to the early Egyptian texts. Egyptian symbology is usually reserved for advanced students, thus you will understand only that what you are ready for. That which is premature will be absorbed for use at a later time.... Remember, the subconscious cannot forget.

Egyptian Parts Of The Soul

KA
The unique identity given by God to each soul. Like a fingerprint or snowflake, there is no other that is the same. The Ka is the individuality. Divine Creator and Creation cannot be isolated.

BA
The medium of the Ka. The virgin Ka reflected to the spirit

world (As above, so below.) It is the spiritual form or body that carries the Ba and dictates the physical phenomena that the Ka uses to express itself. So it can be loosely said that the Ba has two places; one used on the living earth, and one in the beyond.

The Ba in the beyond is not its perfected self, but does exist on a nonphysical plane.

The Ba on its lower level inhabits a physical form of elements to express the Ka. It is not the host/physical body itself. The character of the Ka expresses its uniqueness in the Ba; in other words, the divine intent (Ka) expresses its uniqueness in the divine scheme (Ba). The Ba is the life force of the soul, not the life force of the body, which is called the Sa. The Ba is referred to as "the living," but is not quite that, as seen next.

KHAT

The Khat alone without the Ba is just a combination of elements. As a matter of fact, it is attributed to the shadow of a person (a reflection of their soul) since it has no life of its own but is only a representation of the living Ba.

SA

The Sa is the energy source permeating and enlivening the body. This living energy is called the aura. It has a divine source intended for the "living" only.

HATI OR AB

The energizing of the lower form of life with the spirit, thus making them complete. It is the vital instinctual mechanism of animation and vital physical response. It is the nephesh, also called the "animal soul."

KHIABIT

The Khiabit is the combination of the Khat and Ba. When the Khat is given its Ba, it takes on the individual expression of an emanation of the Creator; it is then called the Khiabit. Without the infusion of the Ba, it is merely an unidentifiable soul dwelling on the physical plane which can cast a shadow. If the Khat is mistaken for a complete body and soul-entity it would be called a vampire, because it has no personna and is an entity.

SAHU

The Sahu is a compilation of all the parts of one's complete soul. It is a representation of the soul in the four Qabalistic worlds and can attain perfection and be like a God, namely Horus. It is the pure form of the complete person (on all levels) as per his original purpose. The Sahu is a state of the soul's perfected self. It exists on the astral plane. Thus it is a reflection of the Khiabit.

SEKHEM

A tool of the Ka providing the ability to grasp what a person can be. It is the way he or she can unite to the "Primal Source." It is the higher self, also known as the "Holy Guardian Angel," occurring in Tiphareth. It is the knowledge of one's Ka! The Sekem is not perfection (Kether). It contains the Khu.

The KHU and the KHABS

The Khu is the "cohabiting glory" also known as the *Shekinah* in ancient Hebraic texts. It is the intertwining of the Godhood with the individual. Yet the Khu contains the link to perfection (total unity with the Ka yielding perfection). This higher creation of the Khu is called the Khabs. It is a soul's attainment to Godhood. Being the Will, the Khabs is located in Daath, and is a reflection of a person's link to the true self.

The Hammemit is the unborn soul traveling about the sun (Khu). (Some traditionalists say it does so for 120 years.) As part of this cycle, it selects the circumstances it will be born to. When Kether and Malkuth unite, birth is proper.

The Tet is referred to also when discussing incarnate life. In brief, it pertains to ultimate perfection of the whole of the individual's growth.

Finally, there is one more word that should be discussed when understanding the Egyptian parts of the Soul. It is Akh. This is the first swirling of manifested spirit from its previous state in the realm of negative existence (where nothingness actually exists). In other words, it is the primal, "divine idea made manifest" from God's seed in the world of existence, during the exact point of this transition.

In summation, an entity is given a substantial, earthbound quality to identify and possess its many parts. A name is given to label or define its identity.

Therefore, the name is its power. It is said that to pronounce it properly is to possess its very soul or at least have access to it. Thus the name releases energy.

This is why a person is shaped by the sounds or connotations of their name.

The ancient Egyptians said that Isis tricked Ra to discover His true name. The ancient Hebrews said that pronouncing the name of God properly would destroy existence.

In ancient Egypt, a common name, a religious name, and an initiated name were given. In the papyrae, the name is called the Ren.

The Aura

What is the aura? What is the body of light? What is the astral body? What is the soul?

The modern spiritual movement has brought into use many new terms and popularized some of the old ones. Many "authorities" throw about such terms they read in books or hear their friends speak; thus these terms have become muddled. Clarified here are the traditional magickal meanings.

The aura is the life-force of the individual. Each individual has a unique aura, as individual as a fingerprint. The aura absorbs the personality of the individual. It radiates from the body in varying amounts depending on how well the individual has learned to control it. It is perceived by few and therefore is little understood.

The individuality is absorbed and carried by other less personal media, for example, a chair you often sit in, your pen, your keys, or money. When a person is emotionally attached to some animate or inanimate object, and he or she has not learned to control his or her aura, then the aura is inadvertently projected into the object. The object then becomes a talisman, an extension of "self." So the aura is absorbed by many objects or persons either by physical proximity or inadvertent energy projection.

When one gives his or her aura out, he or she is literally giving of his or her own self, the "essence," as if he or she were giving a physical part of the brain or other bodily tissue or fluid. The blood is the home of most of the aura and the aura goes with it in transfusions or organ transplants. There are several reported cases where tortured spirits returned through a single microscopic droplet of blood left at the scene of their violent demise. The Egyptians were overwhelmingly concerned with mummification. It kept the aura consolidated in a controlled area, not left about to be defiled by scavengers and or graverobbers, because enough of the aura remains with the corpse that it is still vulnerable.

Moreover, the aura can never be separated from the soul, so the link continues even into the next incarnation.

When one expresses strong feelings such as anger or love, which are subtle yet tangible, the actual identity of the individual is also sent out. Thus the Magickian is discriminating about how emotions are expressed. He or she, as well as others, can be influenced by those who possess his identity. As with lovers whose auras have intermingled: when one is in danger the other feels it. It is important for any spiritual student to keep the aura as clean as possible, i.e., uninfluenced by other auras and their Wills. The purpose of any true spiritual path is to unite with one's true God/ Will. In order to do this, one must dispose of any influence that may either purposely or inadvertently muddle one's identity.

> *The aura is the life-force of the individual.*

Consider the aura a plasticine-elastic substance that can adhere to another person, object, or energy field, sticking to it like rubber or chewing gum. It can stretch very far because it is made of energy and does not have the usual restrictions of matter. It can also change its density or volume.

Some people have accused Mesmer (a German physician of the eighteenth century who was a master of hypnotism, magnetism, and influence—mesmerize is derived from his name) of seducing women by breathing on them and using his aura to create a link with theirs. His detractors further claimed that he would use this aura-link to possess these women without their knowledge and control them.

Thus by creating an aura-link with someone, one possesses a small part of the individual's persona, and an unethical or unknowing person is able to exert an influence on another. This usually happens involuntarily without the knowledge of the giver or the taker.

According to the laws of this current aeon, every person has his or her own individual Will, and to go against it rebukes the laws of Nature. Altering a person's soul and his karma can be dangerous.

Although caring persons may wish to heal others by sending them energy of assorted varieties, often through "white light," this can be harmful to the soul of both sender and receiver. Because the aura link is so thin between individuals, it is permeable and allows any foreign entities to penetrate it. This result has been prominent in almost every case in which follow-ups have been seen. Non-soul entities can possess an unknowing person and weaken him. It requires much expertise and judgment to heal another person. One must have first mastered the forces of Creation and Destruction.

It must be mentioned that the aura is the life force of the corporeal body. Also, ill health is a weakness of the aura. Thus it is absolutely imperative to maintain a clean aura for both physical and spiritual health.

People who have biopsies performed, in which a piece of their living tissue is extracted for examination, are highly subject to aura problems. (However, in certain serious illnesses one must do what is necessary to preserve one's life.) It is, of course, always better to take proper care ahead of time to avoid such situations.

The aura can be kept clean and healthy by certain spiritual exercises. Also, certain vibrational techniques are excellent for revitalizing and detoxifying the aura. These will be taught to the student by his or her Teacher (also Master, etc.)

Diet affects the aura too. For example it can be seen easily how eating meat influences the aura (See page 107, Why Vegetarianism). The animal-life vibration penetrates and de-evolves the human character.

Controlling one's emotions controls the range of the aura. Being careful not to leave traces of one's aura anywhere is also a way to keep it intact. The aura-sealing and revitalizing exercises taught by the Adept are important here. The places that one frequents as well as the people with whom one associates must be carefully chosen, as peoples' auras can easily "rub off."

There are several ways to check one's aura. These are taught by the Spiritual Teacher as an essential part of the foundation of spiritual work.

Astral Projection

Is it through the projection of the aura that we astral project? No. Although the astral body carries with it some of the aura, they are two different things.

The astral plane is a plane of existence other than the physical one. The time continuum is flat and can be traversed. It is a much finer force and vibrates at a higher rate. We exist in that world in our astral bodies as much as we do in our physical bodies. Physical and mental energy occur there just as they do on the physical level but the body vibrates there at a different rate.

We all share the astral plane as we share the physical world. The attachment between the astral and physical world is strong, similar to a mirror, so whatever happens in the physical, effects all beings by going up to the astral plane which we are all a part of. This is the reason why the "group consciousness" changes. At one time there is a particular social mentality which for some reason later changes.

The world is influenced by the astral operations of the Magickian who works on the spiritual level as well as the material level.

Every time a person does any psychic operation at all, entities of energy are created on the astral which of course cannot be destroyed. All the emotions of the populace feed the group consciousness and strengthen certain vibrations.

Magickal operations are serious, and the karma they bear must be realized before anyone uses their occult forces so freely. It doesn't take an Adept to maim or destroy an adversary. Any sloppy self-taught dabbler can direct enough negative energy waves at someone or something.

The semi-secret societies of the true Great White Brotherhood know the damage that can result from psychic attack, and rarely in history have they ever declared war.

It is essential that the student be able to control his counterexistence in the astral world, because his astral actions, in turn, affect the physical world. Every ritual, every act, every emotion, even every thought is absorbed into the astral.

It is not attainment nor a great accomplishment to astrally project (leave the physical body and project one's consciousness along the astral plane). In applied astral projection, one encounters certain experiences and knowledge specifically suited for his needs at that time. Like psychism, arbitrary astral travel is nothing more than entertainment if it does not have a higher purpose. The visions on the astral can be useless or overwhelming. If one is not ready to go where one may end up, the student will short circuit any future astral capability. Thus the projection must be appropriately directed with proper guidance!

> *We all share the astral plane as we share the physical world.*

Since the astral plane is inhabited by humans and their deepest thoughts and experiences, it can be a very disturbing place. Also, the astral plane contains not only human life but other life forms, some friendly, some not. There are specific entities who live there exclusively and do not have a corporeal body. When one first enters there, the astral entities become curious as to who this person is. It is not unlike making a splash in a still pool, while other sun bathers sit and watch in response to the sound. A "new" presence on that plane is keenly perceived. So in the early stages of Magickal practice, various forms of psychic and astral care as well as self-defense and how to maneuver on the astral are taught. The astral plane is an integral tool for the Magickian, thus the ability to use it must be mastered. When the student is ready, the teacher will introduce him to the experience and techniques of astral projection.

Celebrating the Seasons

It is critical that the practitioner, complying with the laws of nature, conduct and utilize energy that comes from the earth and cosmos. In Nature, equilibrium is maintained only through the regular changing of forces called seasons. The Magickian imitates these. In High Magick, the Initiate learns the secrets of tapping such seasonal forces.

The Vernal Equinox (Spring)

This thawing-out process of the earth provides for a slight gradual release of energy from what was for the past six solar months basically inert; locked up but developing.

The earth is freed and opened up. But aid is required to draw this life force up. Here again, mankind, the dominant species appointed to watch over the elements of the planet Earth, must assist them in their growth and quality as per the master plan.

Mankind feels the effect of the transition releasing him from the inertness of life. All things change this day.

We celebrate the source of all life—the sun—rising to provide once more. The darkest night is all over and sunlight starts its reign. Concurrently, the initiates partaking in an equinox ritual have their aura "charged." This goes for their Magickal Order as well. The initiate's part in the scheme of Nature is refortified.

The Summer Solstice (Summer)

The particular force found around this time, referred to as "midsummer," is for all the planet to partake of.

All vegetation absorbs the life force. It is drawn up and stored by the planet. It is truly nature's day! Certain consolidating practices are done for "the whole." Absorption is high then, and Magickians all over the world help raise creation to perfection.

The battery of the planet is thus fortified by the initiates' rituals on this day. Individuals collectively perform to help manifest these cosmic forces. By such union, the Creator and Creation merge within them. On this day the practitioners of rituals receive certain experiences that will influence their future growth. Thus one should know what to do for his own development.

Man is only a reflection of another, much greater system. So by fortifying that system with positive energies, it will feedback positively. That is where the Magickal path differs from others. The feast is for the forces of nature, not the manifestation caused by those forces (i.e., mere planetary changes such as weather, flowers, sunlight, snow, etc.).

The Autumnal Equinox (Fall)

In September the earth receives its last charge of life. It is then, consequently, time to reflect on what has taken place. The Earth is put at peace, and during this reflecting period we calculate the upcoming energies and anticipate what preparations for the dark winter are to be made, new plans established. Allocations are made. Ones quality for this part of the year is set.

The Winter Solstice (Winter)

In December we celebrate the winter solstice. Preparation is made for the upcoming season, and things get ready to be "reborn." A newness is ever present. Any latent forces that were set in motion earlier become more formed and defined, ready to be molded and utilized as their growth culminates. The energy at this time results from the seeds that were planted earlier. The fortification and establishment of man are the energies established during the winter solstice. The indwelling of Spirit within man is emphasized.

All religions celebrate these ancient seasonal rites, acknowledging the esoteric forces of Magick. They do so, however, in slightly different ways, using different names, allegorical myths and slightly altering the dates as they see fit.

PART THREE

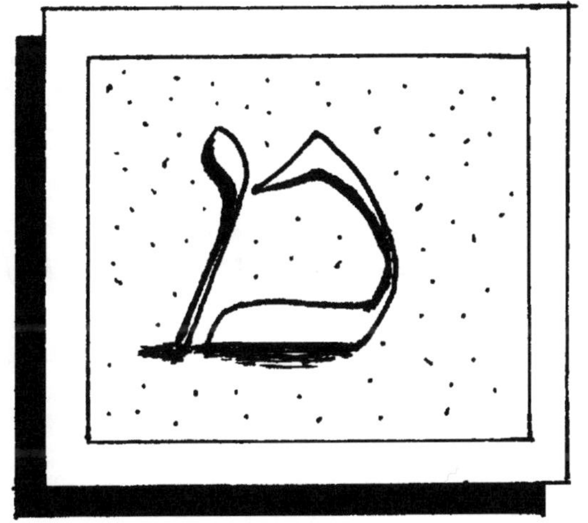

"No one should start thoughtlessly down the path of the arcane sciences, for once one starts he must persevere to the goal. Otherwise, he will be lost. Once on the path, a single doubt will produce madness, a single stop will cause a fall, a single attempt to shrink back will plunge the Luckless soul into a bottomless abyss.

You who are now beginning to read this book will be either a king or a madman once you have finished. You can do what you want to with it; you will never hate or forget it. If your heart is pure, it will be a shining torch; if your heart is strong, it will be a weapon in your hand. If your heart is wise, it will become still wiser. But if your heart is base, this book will be hell fire to you; it will brand your soul and weigh your conscience with eternal sorrow and restlessness."

—Eliphas Levi, in the Rituel de La Haute Magie

"In Practice"

What the Student of Enlightenment Can Expect

The most useful piece of information the student is given, which he or she will have a long time to work on, is simple: the only thing the student knows is that he or she knows nothing. When a student realizes this wisdom, then wisdom begins. When the student attains to adepthood, then he or she understands that he or she knows nothing, but this profound state takes time.

Although we see, we do not know if it's real. Probably the most common mistake is assumption, projecting one act to follow another, e.g., "I know that store has the book because I saw it there yesterday." The student "knew" because he saw the book there yesterday, yet today the book may be sold out. Every person making the transformation to the magickal life must discard this pattern of intellectualization.

Previously in this book the reader is warned never to attempt to see through the eyes of the Adept, because just when you think you know enough to see, you are led through the path of illusion and will see through the eyes of the fool, or even worse. Never be misled by the ego to think you know another person, or even yourself for that matter. And to think you know a thing is just as absurd, because someone else "knows" it to be just the opposite of what you "know," so the knowledge must be wrong somewhere! The student of Magick is taught to unite with things and become one with them. Only then can knowledge be true.

So the learned ego of assuming you know by self-found conclusions instead of perception of any kind is the first thing that has to go if you want to understand reality. This is one of the first lessons that the Adept must teach in order for the student to understand. It is interesting to note how much more faith the arrogant ones have in their own "knowledge" than in what their own teacher directs them to do, until the tower topples and the student realizes that his teacher has taught him by allowing him to experience his "knowledge" as illusion rather than tell him about it. However, when the student's mistakes could lead them to harm, the teacher will prevent such experimental training.

> *Never be misled by the ego to think you know another person, or even yourself for that matter.*

A certain type of faith in the system one chooses is required, for the teacher who represents that system has the same faith in the student as the student for him. That faith is based on demonstrative performance and not on what the leader of that system explains to you through reason. It is reason (the habit of rationalizing) itself i.e., the ego that must be reformed into perception in the enlightenment process.

The student should recognize through his or her own experiences an ability to cause change. The forces that govern will always test and titillate the student and allow him or her to react. The gods only reveal themselves to those who have undertaken action to seek them; not to students who require God make its presence known first! One never tests the gods! One must be deserving before the Gods provide their special gifts.

The student who is dedicated to utilizing his or her higher self without lusting for an intermediary result performs unconditionally. But one who undertakes this work for easy results will never see them. Our work takes a long time and even then perfection might never be reached. There is in fact no "instant" enlightenment. Beware of entities offering the quick route; don't be attracted to *unbalanced* rewards.

Some people are happily willing to attend college for four years to learn to do a job, but when they're told it takes time to learn the secrets of the universe they become disenchanted. If you don't have time, turn your attention to other endeavors. To initiate or confer power prematurely leads to devastating experiences. One must control the self before one can control even higher forces; this principle can not be overly stressed.

The course of study for the magickal art is a true one, that is, it is for a higher purpose, not for entertainment. Although it is enjoyable, to say the least, it is much more than a hobby. So it is best not to make formal commitments until the privilege is suggested by the teacher. There is no necessity for such obligation until you are fit enough to belong (as an integral part) to that system.

Nature works so that when you are deserving and have become a fit receptacle, She will come to you. Powers come by attraction of a similar force. Like a magnet, only a suitable force can attract them.. They will seek and find that force when least expected. Even if one were to try to avoid them, these powers would find one. And one who looks for them will repel them.

After a short while of practicing Magick the aspirant notices certain abilities. In the properly taught school, these are recognized as tools that are developed along the way. They should not be mistaken for attainment of the final result[1] (although the lay person will consider them supernatural), or one may never attain but just have subordinate powers and no more.

One should expect the tests that pull one away from improvement at the most auspicious times. Often they are rational excuses made by the Nephesch (the "animal soul" which restricts personal evolution). Often they are really legitimate, and the aspirant will have to perform, not just talk about spirituality. The tests aren't easy, but be thankful that the gods even

---

1. Psychism is a good example of this.

see you fit to quality for them—if you were never tested how could you demonstrate or perform?

Attempting to outwit nature by improvising and amending Her tried and true practices with new practices that seem sensible at the time leads to disappointment and failure (see "Path Hopping"). If you have faith in a course of spirituality and have formed a usable bond between yourself and that system of nature which will open you to higher things, why try to improvise? The ego is what prompts such improvisations. Just when you think you know better than the system you are studying, is when you get burned.

Don't be afraid to fail (not fall). Failure is relative and the teacher knows of your failure before you do, so he will either help you to avoid it or allow it to happen if it will be a good learning experience for you. The teacher will never reject the student who shows his intentions and knowledge are still earnest, even if he fails and fails! The teacher takes no one personally because he has learned to destroy the ego. He has replaced it with the love of the universe. There is no good or bad side of the teacher to get on. You are always before him so he can see you and address you properly. He offers his love for his students merely for the price of their sacrificing illusion. This is true love.

Relax and enjoy the whole of the magickal experience. Although discovering your Will is a serious job, it is not restricting. A course of spirituality is designed to give you the facility to eliminate restrictions of the true Will. Approaching Magick or spirituality too cautiously is like approaching love too cautiously. You'll never be able to appreciate its true bliss. Dive in and let spirit be your guide, not the intellect! Don't worry. Your teacher will temper your overindulgence if necessary. Make it the most beautiful experience in the world. The morose stringency of Magick or the occult is only needed in Hollywood.

Before you go on to deeper practices, master the basics you were taught. No matter how much you think the preliminaries are unnecessary or boring, forge ahead. If your Magick is not fun, you are not mastering it and have more to go. Once mastered, the most mundane exercises are ecstatic. That is how you become ready to go further. Examine the reasons why you are or aren't using certain exercises to their fullest benefit. Be objective. Keep the natural novelty alive, lest you allow the scatteredness of your mind to grow. Build a strong foundation first. It is necessary.

Give and take. Enjoy these experiences. Be part of what you're doing if you want to accelerate the evolution of your soul. Don't fool yourself. The more of yourself you put into the system you're using, the more of an energy link will be formed. Don't believe, however, that this is a quick way to progress. It only makes it one step easier. The endurance and expertise are still up to you!

Question your old thoughts and spiritual practices if they are not able to manifest change in your life! This is why you're doing what you're doing!

In this aeon everyone's Will is different and no system can teach all of its students in the same way, at the same pace, with the same material. You must literally be taught individually and you can only take one road at a time to the source. Your intellect will only be a time-consuming stumbling block to be surmounted. Are you more devoted to your work or your spirituality; your social commitments and obligations, your image maintenance; your art; or you Will? Do you want to just learn to control your life more; serve the new aeon; learn the mysteries and be part of an organization? Do you want Adepthood? Initiation? To what degree do you want to grow? Determine your goals. Whatever they are they must be real; not just rhetoric or what you think your teacher wants to hear. Not all must attain to the priesthood! Not all must be limited to just learning things about themselves without moving onto mastery!

Be happy with your goal and let nothing stop you. If so, you have failed and will either start again or run away in despair. Make a plan to reach your goal; it can be modified if necessary. Tell your spiritual teacher and he will guide you appropriately.

Magickal forces are tangible and powerful, so the aspirant must be taught to experience and control them slowly and carefully.[2] It is not difficult to invoke nature's energies, but to control them requires great expertise and discipline. Accurate knowledge is a necessity.

The aspirant has in his possession a most effective tool for

---

2. The laws of nature will work for you, if you work with them. Look at a fulcrum, a lever based on the law of gravity. Depress this lever, and it can lift tons. This is an act of Magick.

manifesting hidden power.[3] The way to this universal power is to go within, but is no more self-taught than any other power of the self. Your spiritual teacher, whose level of attainment allows him to guide and teach you, will probe the heart of creation and allow you to utilize it properly. The spiritual teacher devotes himself to those aspirants who are committed to learning. It is his job to provide true divine experiences to those he accepts. The criteria for selection is usually not the aspirant's attainment, but rather his deeds. Every person has his own level of development, but not all are meant for grand attainments in this lifetime. The true teacher sees the aspirant's potential.

> *Dive in and let spirit be your guide, not the intellect!*

In dealing with your spiritual teacher, remember this: If you yourself wish one day to be a master, do not copy the Will of your teacher. Let him inspire you, but do not try to be a carbon copy of his or anyone else's Will. This is one reason why the true master reveals little of himself. He does not want clones but rather wants his students to do their own Wills. He will also attempt to demonstrate his humanness to his students by acting so candidly that there should be no difference between his character in front of people and when he is alone. It is not easy for the teacher to do things that will keep others from replicating his identity but he will always try, even sometimes portraying a character his students may not care for if he feels they are attempting to copy his Will. His admission and demonstration of his own errors are essential to his difficult job. Most students, however, will establish this discrimination after a while.

Those who have found a true Adept (which is rare indeed) must value him. There is a divine reason why he has found you ("When the student is ready the master will appear"). This means you must respect your opportunity to study under him and think carefully before you let some temporary stimulation make you stray from his guidance; it is priceless.

For those of you who have studied other paths before set-

---

3. You are not the power; you only contain it. The power is Kether/God etc.

tling on a valid teacher, don't project your fears or bad experiences with your past teachers on him anymore than he should project his bad experiences with other students on you. Do not be so afraid to immerse yourself in the system he shows you; he will not go too fast for your own good. Make use of the opportunities he offers you.

It is devastating to see so many prospectively good students burn themselves out and never be able to develop because of the emotional experiences that their past teachers have left with them. How closed they have become, sometimes not to blossom in this life. If it is difficult due to your trauma not to equate the intentions of a charlatan with the intentions of a true Adept, you must open up rather than shut the door of enlightenment and do it for your own spiritual good (which will reflect to the world of course) and let the forces of karma do their justice to he who blasphemes divine knowledge and privilege.

There are so many different paths to spiritual attainment; what if a student chooses the wrong one? To flounder about without ever choosing to be committed to any path (because one is afraid to make a mistake) is the greatest wrong of all. It is one's Will to choose what will teach him what he needs to know at the time. The Holy Order of The Winged Disk teaches that a certain amount of truth can be found in every tradition, and we therefore recognize all of them (except the charlatans, of course). The stories are all the same; it is just the format of the characters and the methods of providing experiences for attainment that change.

Even though you may not agree with another's approach to God, you must respect it because he is doing hard work just like you, and it is no man's place to judge the path to God unless one is a God, and even then, God offers many ways. Never tell another of your spirituality as if he or she should do what you are doing to find God! This is an attempt to distort another's Will and is the practice of the dark side, no matter how well-intentioned the efforts may be. A person is in a certain place because this is what he must do at that time. You are at your level or place because you are ready for that.

Thus it is that a true path of spirituality will never attempt to recruit others. People must find their correct spiritual path when they are ready.

Our spiritual Order, The Winged Disk, practices overcoming obstacles to the true Will. Thus it is suggested that if you feel someone you know might benefit from our tradition, you must recommend that which you yourself were first instructed to read—perhaps Dion Fortune's *Mystical Qabalah,* or this book. Allow that person to pursue the path or not, according to his or her own feelings. Do not try to persuade! Coercion is used by some modern systems who prey on the weak and must depend on always increasing their followers.

> *Often the aspirant wants power but is afraid of it when it comes.*

To reduce your spirituality to intellectualism by speaking about it to others only reinforces the ego and pushes your own progress even further out of reach. So be silent like the Godchild Harpocrates. Be reverent of your spirituality. It is not meant to be discussed and to do so simply puts you in the heap of spiritual has-beens. This is very common among dabblers.

Even among your fellow students, controlling idle chatter is essential, and one who is not even able to attempt that has no chance of harnessing anything else! Those who have moved along our path with apparent dominion and attainment are the most silent.

Sometimes a students gets scared because he realizes that he has come in contact with a real Adept and sees the awesome forces of reality presented before him. Because he has never seen anything like this before, he immediately draws back in fear not realizing that the Adept is really in control of these forces. Recognize that the unknown is not dangerous when the Adept is by your side.

Often the aspirant wants power but is afraid of it when it comes. This narrow-minded approach shows that his faith was not real, and in the words of the ancient traditions, "Each person is given the opportunity once in a lifetime...and that's all. If they reject it they may never be given the chance again in that lifetime until the next time around." This seems to be a particular mechanism of these forces of nature, and every true Adept will concur with this axiom. (To stumble, even to fail, and try again is not construed as the rebuke stated above.) Results only come when the student has laid the foundation for their arrival; so don't think that results are external to yourself, like watching a movie. Rather, they are a direct function of the energy stirred and invoked by the student.

In dealing with the Adept, let it be emphasized again that his energy field or presence may feel awesome to the point of intimidation, but it is just the forces of nature that surround him as he walks, not any chaotic or negative force. Respect those forces just as he does, but allow them to know you! And deep within their center is the heart of the master which is love. Don't misinterpret his power as wrath. Conversely, his power is love and that is why he has embraced you to study under him.

Destruction of the ego is the first step in opening the gates to enlightenment. It is taught in the old system that each person must learn that the false images made up in the mind will prevent the perception of reality. This is in part the ego that each system attempts to destroy—egocentricity as well as the falsification process. Often the student must accept this until he no longer cares about his false image and stands figuratively naked, exposed to ego-destruction in front of those whom he wanted to impress. So be prepared to have your ego broken if you want to be taught the real harnessing powers.

Ego feeds illusion. Magick is the inducing of reality. The two, ego and Magick do not mix. If the student is robbed of the opportunity for his "pride to take a fall" he may also be robbed of other magickal procedures the teacher can provide. So when the teacher treats you in this way it is a valuable experience. The student must never allow himself to feel that the teacher is subject to uncontrolled moods or prejudices against him; a true teacher is above personal likes or dislikes of those whom he must care for and learns to love them all. It is the false masters who will always make you feel good. Never attempt to think you know what the Adept knows or feels. He reveals only what you should know and his tests and teaching methods from your experiences are the reason why you study under him. To simply be informed of the way without experiencing it means that you can replace the function of the teacher with a book.

So don't profane your teacher by assuming that you know his motivations. He sees things that you don't. You will realize that only after attainment and mastering vanity.

Failures result from the stronghold of the dominant ego. Your rewards will result from the progress you make in battling and overcoming ego. Although these techniques may be construed by those not on the magickal path, as cruel and demeaning, know it is not so. The close feeling and respect that the teacher has at all times is for those who ardently wish to expand themselves, and is beyond measure. No matter how much the student has to labor, the true teacher is there by his side at all times, guiding, caring, praying for him as if he were his own child. The student's welfare is never out of the teacher's thoughts. Now you see why it takes so long and why so few can become spiritual teachers; they must at all times, under all circumstances, love those who have chosen them to teach true spirituality. Woe to the teacher who fails to control the weaknesses that should have been mastered in his own training. It is imperative that the teacher and student move as one (though the student is not yet allowed the privilege of seeing how this inner universal mechanism works).

Devotion by the student to his spiritual quest and path is an early task, but even more so the teacher must be absolutely, unconditionally devoted to his student. His students may fail, but as they are not yet masters it can be accepted. But for the Adept it is unpardonable and bears a heavy penalty. Thus it is the student by virtue of his position who needs devotion from the teacher. Rarely does the student realize this, because students are told by those "leaders" who desire followers that devotion is a one-way street, and required of the student only.

The Adept is reality, so learn from him. Like Tarot cards, he is designed to assist your own evolution and is at your disposal. Those powers are not there to "mystify" you. Your teacher will tell you if you go too far.

The final thing that must be stated here is that the student must expect to be given the opportunity of service. Without this, the integral program is incomplete. It is not the act that is important as the way its done. To build just a door lovingly for the betterment of the Great Work is more important than to build a whole temple halfheartedly.

Contrary to the popular opinion that the pyramids of ancient Egypt were built by captive slaves, know that they were built by willing devotees who felt it a great privilege to serve their gods. They wanted to do their part. Their goal was to be chosen to serve. Not all were worthy to work on such a holy project. The opportunity to do the difficult labor needed to build these holy places was something people strived all their lives to be considered worthy of.

A formal study of practical Magick requires:

a) Magical records.

b) Daily practices as well as:

c) Middle term practices.

d) Long term practices.

e) Investigation of the present events caused by past events.

f) The ability to differentiate between truth and illusion, and clarity of mind, which is usually obtained through being taught to understand the self. An absolute objective observer is required.

g) A working knowledge, i.e., intellectual study.

h) Direction. One must have a realistic format for his own quest.

i) The ability to conquer the microcosm/self before further abilities can be attempted.

j) The actual experiences of natural Magick.

k) Devotion. This is the true test of how much one wants to attain. This is based on faith as evidences by the magickal experiences that the teacher leads his students to.

The student must expect to be provided with:

a) A facility in which to learn devotion to spirit by providing service.

b) True mystical experiences.

c) Specific disciplines dispensed by an Adept.

d) Answers to relevant questions.

e) That which will lead him away from judging the spiritual quality of himself or another.

f) That which will provide the student with an effective way of seeing an accurate picture of his true self.

g) The method of approaching and utilizing the knowledge and powers of his higher self (a reflection of perfected soul...a fragment of God).

The Teacher must:

a) Provide all of the above.

b) Not want his students to follow him, but rather his system of enlightenment.

c) Make sure that he never for a moment, rejects a serious student. (When in doubt of a student's worthiness to use the teacher's energy and time, the teacher must give the prospective student certain qualifying disciplines that will allow him to demonstrate his worthiness)

d) Never provide his spiritual services for the sole purposes of gaining personal wealth or personal profit (i.e., selling spirituality). His purpose is to teach his students and further his tradition. And in doing so he establishes a reciprocal link (like all energies that exist in the universe) and will be supported by his students return for such knowledge. He must channel as much funds as possible to the profess house and to support the functions of the Order of which he is a member. It is his job to see the profess-house is provided for thusly.

This etching shows the students wondeful array of wisdom to draw upon in the search for God.

On Silence

It is said that the sage-philosopher Pythagoras required a strict unbroken vow of five years of monitored silence for student-candidates before he would consent to teach them. This mathematical Magickian's philosophy was "moderation in all things." He felt that if one would not give up speech for this relatively short period, one would not be committed to learning.

Throughout the ages, silence has always been a prerequisite to magickal undertakings. As the true tradition decayed into a popular movement, this requirement was relaxed to attract more followers. Some traditions even permitted socializing within the organization to keep their members. However, as with all unrefined human nature, the egos reigned and were allowed to run free, leading others astray. As a result, some fine organizations fell apart or couldn't provide true magickal experiences. Without understanding this most people select a more lenient path that may allows weakness to thrive.

People frequently speak as a defense mechanism so that the

As so nicely explained in Crowley's Aeon card, (formerly called the Judgement card), Harpocrates is Horus the child. He was innocent and silent and the energythat dwells whereever ther is silence.

focus is diverted away from themselves. Magickal attainment demands self-control before other forces can be mastered. "Do with your heart and not your lips" is what separates dabblers from earnest practitioners.

People, by false or inaccurate words, create illusion and deception. By not knowing the power of words, even those who mean well may create destructive energy by their casual speech and disregard for what they say! Thus, harnessing the enormous internal power of the word requires gradual and personal instruction and should not be neglected. The failure rate of would-be Magickians and the number of magickal breakdowns is so large because the victims were not taught this principle and therefore didn't understand it. The Magickian works with the force of reality. Illusion creates dangerous conflict in the psyche and idle words feed illusion.

The old traditions teach such control because words create things on a more subtle plane which then manifest on the earth plane. This even applies to what one thinks. The energy that you transmute from words, like all energy, cannot be destroyed. Yet the Adept knows that one word can create or destroy any phenomenon he manifests, because his control has been so diligently developed that every word is an act of Will. To those not yet trained, it is important to know conversation is usually an act of the ego. Subduing the ego is the biggest task of the earliest stages of spiritual growth, One achieves this in order to see what is hidden behind the veil of ego. A quiet mind will hear the soft "voice of intuition" which is always there but can't be heard over a busy mind.

Superfluously speaking "grounds out" the divine vibration. The word was so powerful in Ancient Egypt that only the high priests were permitted to learn the sacred art of writing, as taught by the god Thoth. Thoth also taught all the gods words in order for them to affect their Magick. The god who reigns in this aeon is Horus who as Harpocrates is the Lord of Silence.

Imagination or Mystical Experience

The beginning student often asks the important question "What is real mystical experience and what is my imagination?"

Perceiving higher dimensions requires receptiveness of the mind to "other things" (i.e., non-ordinary thought patterns and experiences). This state is called imagination. Imagination is not self-created but, as explained by the Qabalah, comes from a part of the soul beyond the intellect. Imagination is actually perception! Above and behind imagination is the single force of creation known as Spirit or "God", which is even further removed from the creative part of the mind!

Every great revelation has come from a highly developed state of "imagination". Illusions come from the intellect, not from the real imagination of Spirit (creative mind),

> *Imagination should be nurtured, not demeaned.*

which people seem to discount as falsehood!

The aspirant should never doubt that what he or she sees is emanating from the limitless mind (imagination); in fact, the aspirant should do exercises to break the limits of intellect and perceive images transmitted from the higher self. Mistaking imagination as self-made illusion is the obstacle that can destroy an aspirant's observations of truth/reality. Imagination should be nurtured, not demeaned (see the Fool card).

When a prophet "sees" into the future, he bypasses the intellect and taps into his imagination which he values as another level of reality.

It has been said that imagination is the key to attainment, for if one doesn't have the ability to visualize, one cannot perceive the mysteries which are invisible to the physical eyes! One must go beyond the intellect in order to accept deep realizations.

Every great prophet, tarot reader, seer, diviner etc. tosses away the intellect during their divinations in order to allow the imagination to indwell, because the imagination recognizes data the ordinary mind considers impossible. What you cannot perceive, you cannot conceive.

Expect to divest yourself of illusion on the Hermetic path. The Magickian's power comes from the one and only source of all created power. You can utilize that power only by uniting with it through its hidden mystical nature (known as the mysteries to the uninitiated). It is not possible to understand the physics of nature through mere intellectual comprehension. (Ask Einstein!)

Expect also to divest yourself of your self-created accumulated ego-knowledge. This procedure requires humility, not the common falsehood of humbleness or ethical reverence. Having a perspective to reality is important here.

The higher forces of nature challenge and provoke the intellect which lusts to arrogantly explain them. Especially with the unknown the intellect strains to defend its inability to rationalize divine phenomena. For example, a very popular, widely accepted holy book says that God made man in his own image. Translated that means one's perfected self is really an image form, not the visual manifestation of body and five senses that man thinks he is (ego). Your personality and body are only expressions of your soul. They are not your soul. The experience of soul occurs by imagining, not thinking.

Illusions, dreams, imagination, fantasy—what are the differences? Illusion is a false experience or perception. Its material is not real. Dreams are the language of the inner mind or subconscious for expressing real material that the conscious mind chooses not to handle. Everything in a dream is an important symbol. (Even in prophetic dreams the message is often rejected by the conscious mind.) Imagination is an extremely deep insight into reality that goes beyond the common process of rationalization. So when you think your experience has been "just" your imagination, know that you have opened the door to a world known as "true mystical experience." Fantasy is the expression of imagination in any deliberate act to either fulfill a desire or to express an inner drive.

Intuition is perception beyond the five recognized senses. Intuition detects reality, whether past, present, or future.

If you cannot imagine, you cannot open up to intuition because they both require synthesizing information. One must be receptive to that which appears irrational because the intellect, the mundane operation of the mind, cannot comprehend intuition. Letting go of the restrictions of the sensible intellect invokes intuition/imagination.

So, what is real mystical experience? It is a magickal experience incurred as part of a spiritual path for the purpose of obtaining wisdom of the self that cannot be conveyed by intellectual means or someone else's personal experience. It can occur through the guidance and direction provided by your path when you are ready and according to your level of preparedness.

The understanding of Magick cannot be taught in words. The method that are taught to bring one to that understanding must be concise. People can often console you, teach you, inspire you, comfort you, thrill you, etc. Often such interactions are mislabeled as "mystical experiences." A true mystical experience, however, is beyond uniting with an intellectual concept or idea—it is a union with Diety. It must not be confused with:

a. Illusionary experience interpreted as a divine act.

b. An ordinary experience that would occur during the course of daily life but might have an "other wordly" feel to it.

For example, contrary to what some New Age people believe, that hallucinogenic drugs open one up to the divine source, they in fact open one up only to a chemical malfunction of the brain cells of perception. What one experiences is the effect that the chemicals dictate, rather than how the higher self would experience something. It is much like watching someone else have an experience, and you are merely a witness.

In another case, one may think of a red bird and then one appears. If one lives in an area where such birds habitate, this is still an ordinary probability. In another common occurrence, one can receive advice, sympathy, or simple philosophy from a religious leader and mistake it for a true mystical experience. Group gatherings where a leader speaks can make one feel good, inspired, consoled, or assured of promises of future blessings. However, this is similar to the soothing effects of psychotherapy, but again it isn't mystical experience.

Often people try to rationalize or justify acting on a strong impulse or idea by attributing it to intuition, again saying "It just feels right!" Although this can be a sign of getting in touch with one's higher self, it is not mystical experience. Only when one is capable of opening up to supernatural phenomenon can one have a true mystical experience.

> *The understanding of Magick cannot be taught in words.*

Resistance

What happens when spiritual growth begins to occur? Things change and that which couldn't be done yesterday can be done today. Concurrently, the aspirant also encounters obstacles and subtle diversions, which can lead to success or failure depending on how they are handled. These obstacles are forms of resistance. The Nephesch (the animal soul) which was in control for so long, begins to get tamed through the magickal practices. It will then start to resist and will try to maintain control by finding ways to challenge the aspirant, thus creating illusionary yet intensely felt inner conflicts, large or small. It is this animal part of the soul that is contradictory to the individual's human evolution. In the nephesch's compulsion to hold on to its control, distortions of the Will occur, which seem quite appropriate and relevant at the time. How the aspirant responds to these instances of temptation determines the extent of her progress on the path.

The intellect can justify and explain any action and can convince one that there are good reasons for doing something that is actually contrary to one's own well being. Although intellect is inferior to the Will, it can make illusions seem real. These illusions, which always make sense at the time, include laziness, faithlessness, suspicion, inertia, and fear of giving up the false sense of the self (ego).

So when treading any spiritual path, one will be confronted by such tests, which actually indicate that the aspirant is making progress. If this were not the case, why would the Nephesch assert its presence? The assertion of the higher self over the lower self teaches, strengthens, and empowers the higher Will. Succumbing to the lower self makes the true Will weaker. This is why one needs almost daily personal contact and instruction from an Adept on this path. Every course of action for "activating" the higher self is individualized. However, one fundamental for all is to never make an enemy of the nephesch. Only an Adept's skill can show the magickal aspirant how to keep the peace. Every path of enlightenment must be capable of handling this volatile and inevitable situation to ensure a true and safe empowerment and realization of the true Will.

Even a psychotherapist can vouch that when clients' defense mechanisms are being challenged, through touching on something that makes them see their destructive motivations, yawning, boredom, sleepiness, forgetfulness, or other avoidance techniques usually set in. Thus the client tries to "escape." This may happen to the student of enlightenment if he accepts these interferences as Will. Logic and rationale supply him with all the reasons he needs to take him away from his disciplines and practices. This defense mechanism will operate only when the true Will is starting to assert itself and "tame" the illusion.

To minimize the frequency of these episodes of resistance, one must develop endurance and have true dedication and a desire for learning and growth. The student must look for the specific underlying cause of suppressing of his true Will (not just his desires). Then he will be more able to assert it, because the Will is stronger than the nephesch. His spiritual teacher will guide him accordingly.

It is man's nature to learn and grow. You must know your exact spiritual goals and what is required to obtain them. Know that when the lower self becomes fidgety, it is a normal reaction to the healing process, like the itching of a wound.

Although endurance is necessary, placing unrealistic demands on oneself can cause short-circuiting. Resistance peaks and will eventually pass if one has spent enough energy preparing for it. This means that you can win one battle between light and darkness. As you progress on the path there will be other episodes. At any time in your life that the nephesch is allowed control, even for an instant (and usually when you least expect it), it could undo your progress.

Since your tests of Will are likely to occur when you have made certain strides, welcome these challenges with enthusiasm, for they mean you have done something right. Lack of confidence will hold your progress back. Resistance is a self-imposed restriction that will attempt to pull you down in life whenever you try to break those habits or actions that keep you from your true self.

To fully overcome this is in itself an act of deep Magick, for what is Magick but the ability to cause change in anything if it is in accordance with the Will.

Now one can begin to see why one must master himself in order to have mastery over "circumstances." Circumstances are always self-created or self-sustained. This is a law of Nature despite any rationale analysis to the contrary!

The Hierophant and Priestess

Man (meaning humanity; both male and female) is a creation and model of the universe. Being part of existence, mankind shares the same properties. These forces of nature exist within each individual.

When an Adept becomes a spiritual teacher he is called a Hierophant, and she a Priestess. Both relate the forces of Creator to the world by personifying and utilizing the powers of nature. Not all magickal groups have the luxury of both a physical Hierophant and Priestess. However every group must contain the hierophant and priestess energy. This is mandatory.

To ascertain the higher and profound particulars of the Hierophant and Priestess, the total concept must be established.

Both officers "imitate" nature. Both are serious, respected representatives of God. Although many appoint themselves to such high attainment, these offices are very rarely bestowed when genuine. The aspirant understands that God is all the "gods" and "goddesses" together. Those who regard only the "goddess" or "god" are ill-informed and invite severe imbalances.

The phenomena the Magickian works with are both active and passive. Both are essential and complement each other. Together they comprise the whole. Too much activity denies the Magickian from being able to receive that which is invoked. Too much passivity denies the Magickian from actively pursuing that which can and should be obtained. The current intellectual concepts of *active* or *passive* are merely foolish social stigmas.

The attained Magickian has properly established the inner balance of his or her nature. Such balance is explained in the Magus card. The officer who operates alone is able to invoke and receive, but when there is the availability of having both a hierophant and priestess, they can operate as one single unit.

162

This situation is explicitly shown in the Art card.

The Hierophant is the point (microcosm) within the circle (macrocosm) that is the Priestess. He is activity while she is manifestation. He desires to expand, radiating outward in all directions. She desires to consolidate to a finite. The Hierophant disseminates life into the Priestess who will develop it into one single form.

The Hierophant is the expounder of mysteries. Yet no one may receive mother nature's mysteries unless Isis (the primeval goddess) consents to raise her "veil" which ordinarily conceals these mysteries. Thus the priestess is the true initiator, and the hierophant the true teacher. The aspirant must be deemed worthy to be granted entrance to the circle.

The question often arises concerning the hierophant and priestess's relations with the aspirants (students, members, etc.). The Hermetic system teaches that he is the embodiment of wisdom while she is the expression of understanding. As the hierophant force invokes an energy, the priestess force manifests it. Together they are like opposite poles of a battery, and in the conjoining of the two, this "battery" of Magick is developed. The aspirant in such a situation is fortunate. Neither officer (in this system) engages in sexual relations with the student. Why? Because outside affiliations can drain the battery. (Some organizations differ in this regard and find it beneficial to engage the officers with the members during some ceremonies.)

In the upper levels of Hermetic magickal attainment, however, the position of two complementary priestesses is recorded. It was said that these

> *The Hierophant is the expounder of mysteries.*

represented the Maerti twins (Isis, life force, and her twin sister Nephthys, the giver of form to that life force).

Briefly here is the formula: There are four worlds or levels of existence. The first is the Divine/active/secret. The second is creative/passive/amorphous. The third is intellectual/active/cognizant. The fourth is physical/passive/receptive. God is the first world. One priestess is the senses of the second world. Her compliment is the priest of the third world, of knowledge. The bearer of manifestation is the other Priestess of the fourth world. (For those of you knowledgeable in Alchemy, this is the marriage and transmutation formula of the court cards.) The master of the lodge chooses whether or not to employ this historical system. Often this is not feasible in today's modern world.

What does each officer do?

The Hierophant teaches the literal/applied facets of Magick and is the link between "esoteric" and "exoteric".[1] The Priestess instills those intangible mysteries. While he is accessible to very few, she is the expression of all that is mysterious. As he is the supreme interpretation of the sun, she is the supreme interpretation of the moon. He contains the Magick; she contains nature's mystery!

It is said, again according to the ancient texts, that no one approaches the Hierophant without first approaching the priestess. As he is the disseminator of mysteries, she is that which receives the seeker, and is therefore, the link to him and those mysteries.

Thus both officers nurture the student in their different ways. The hierophant is the custodian of the heart of the organization and its "link to the superiors." She is the custodian of its relationship to the outer world. He anoints and passes on power. She cleanses and builds. He charges the form that she gives. The organization uses him to bring forth and her to admit that which the organization wills.

In our Hermetic system of ceremonial western Magick, attainment occurs by mastering the Sephiroth on the Tree of Life. The hierophant (also called priest) must be master of at least the first six Sephiroth, inclusive of the sixth (Tiphareth). Tiphareth means "balance," and is also the state where one has knowledge and use of his or here own true Will. Connecting the Sephiroth are twenty-two "paths" represented by the tarot trumps. The paths symbolize the forces of nature which manifest change. For example, the rising of the Nile is a change providing irrigation. Yet the force that causes it to rise is unseen. The spreading of its waters can be called the priest force. The reason it rises can be called the priestess force. The two offic-

---

1. Inner hidden working of nature and its outer physical manifested existence, respectively.

ers are proficient in the balance of both.

The Priestess force is attributed to two places on the Tree of Life. The "outer" Priestess is the physical embodiment of the ultimate priestess—the goddess, mother nature herself. She is attributed to the intersection of the two paths assigned to the Art card and the Tower card. Art is the process of transcendence using that which the priest has invoked. The Tower is the connecting path between Hod (intellect) and Netzach (senses). The "inner" Priestess corresponds to the 11th path on the Tree, directly linking god/Kether and the supernal triangle to the Hierophant.

Students approach the mysterious lady who symbolizes nature to request entrance to the chamber of the Hierophant. The hierophant may consent to teach them or not. Ironically, the mysteries he represents are those of nature herself that originally welcomed the aspirant!

Initiation

Initiation is an invitation to unite with the Supreme Force that opens the door to higher knowledge. It "gives notice" to the forces of creation that an Adept will properly and responsibly guide a candidate on his spiritual quest; thus the link is formed. The oath of initiation taken by the candidate is serious and binding. The Hierophant establishes and provides this link to the trustworthy initiate, but he must never be confused with the Creator.

The Hierophant must be available for the needs of his students at all times. He also takes on the karma of his students whether they fall or attain from the carefully guided path of enlightenment. The true teacher of spirituality, therefore, cannot effectively lead thousands, as he could not knowing the individual lives and circumstances of his students. It would then be up to the student to initiate himself. This is unfortunately a common problem, where a spiritual teacher often doesn't even know the names of his students.

Initiation facilitates the removal of illusion and unnatural human restriction, making the Will more accessible. Although formal initiation is available to very few, all will encounter the opportunity to find their proper spiritual path at some point in their lives, for it is human nature to evolve, grow, and change. Thus, initiation occurs at a different time for each person/soul, although this opportunity may not be recognized as such.

Formal initiation occurs when the initiate is granted the power of any sephirah (See Qabalah). The hierophant grooms the student as a conduit for the sephirotic forces to flow into; as a result, he acquires a profound universal energy which can be used constructively or destructively, if the initiate is not careful and prudent. Thus, the initiate is instructed to be aware of both the angels and the demons of each level of attainment. The forces of nature are constant (electricity can either provide light or electrocute). It is the job of each person to comply with nature's laws. The creator does not grant initiation freely.

It can only be conveyed through one who has accurately conducted and demonstrated control of such forces. (Strengthening the self so as not to attract hostile forces is an early prerequisite of initiation.) One can not initiate oneself and freely be given the ultimate gift of divine attainment and knowledge.

Early initiations up the Tree of Life include the lessons of endurance. The limitations that are imposed on the self are targets of the preliminary work to be undertaken so they may be overcome. Moderate endurance is fine for the moderate man or woman, but Magick requires of the practitioner mastery over ordinary restrictions and the ability to rise above circumstances and obstacles in order to attain one's purpose in life. Thus, initiation provides the "tools" but most importantly, teaches one how to use them.

> *The Hierophant must be available for the needs of his students at all times.*

It is said that the reason people choose to be on this earth is to rectify their past karma and thus find a way to fulfill and express their true Will. No one is born to remain in a stagnant state. Thus humanity develops as a result of each individual's growth, overcoming their weaknesses instead of being ruled by them.

Initiation is not the solemn, morbid sacrifice that some perceive it to be. The rare honor of initiation deserves great respect. It feels joyous, satisfying, and stimulating. But these are mere words made by man for a divine event. Thus no words can adequately convey that feeling accompanying initiation. Perhaps it is best that way. Only the experience can reveal how it makes you feel.

Initiation actually brings you closer to your true Will, although the complete Will of the soul is often not recognized at that one moment. The act of approaching the Will must not be mistaken for uniting with the Will.

The rite of initiation opens and directs a flow of energy that the initiate has never experienced before, but initiation is not entirely devotional service. However, some organizations recruit members by easily bestowing what they choose to call initiations, then requiring service from the initiate. Service is only one part of being an initiate. True initiation works like the yin/yang of the universe; one should offer devotion and receive visible results. Initiation means that one has pledged to lead a lifestyle devoted to a particular process for one's spiritual growth. It also means that one must study the occult sciences through the practices, tasks, disciplines, etc., that one is assigned. Initiation should enhance the life of the initiate using occult forces, so that over time he can experience fulfillment and excellence in his life.

The only other binding commitments are to maintain secrecy and to attempt to avert circumstances which would put the initiate in a position where he can regress. A true initiated course of enlightenment moves at the aspirant's own pace and allows him to have true magickal experiences relative to his Will, not a standard program in which the aspirant develops blind faith or memorized learning.

Initiation provides a system of experiences leading to understanding of the Qabalah. The Tree of Life contains a link called the priestess force that opens the initiate to the Godhead as he was taught by the hierophant. It is an essential part of magickal attainment. Knowing the polarities on the Tree is important for initiation. Until that time, any knowledge of the Qabalah can only be intellectual.

The Mechanics of Initiation

An initiate learns "the secrets." One is not capable of being initiated into a sephirah until one has made certain preparations, such as harmonizing with those sephirotic forces. The initiatory experiences and exercises given in preparation for each state of enlightenment are numerous. Some are without the candidate's knowledge! Others are deliberate "assignments."

One must conquer all the forces of a sephirah before one is initiated into that grade. Simply experiencing those forces does not mean that one has conquered them. All people, initiated or not, often experience the sephirotic forces but may not master them. The holy secrets of each grade are revealed during and after the initiatory tests and tasks. This is the way of learning in the western hermetic system.

As stated earlier, initiation takes many forms. Sometimes initiations are disguised thus giving the candidate the opportunity to act without any motivation for results. This eliminates those who strive for status or reward only and forget the goal of spiritual enlightenment. It is critical that the initiator makes sure the candidate is ready. Spirit gives or takes according to one's actions, not one's intentions, overtures, or words. Spirit does not succumb to human sentimentality. The aspirant must prove himself genuinely fit.

Before beginning formal magickal training, some circumstances or events may have been presented in the individual's life as tests to see if he was ready for a teacher. (The candidate may never have known was happening.) Thus, some hardships in life might be karmic[1] but some may be initiatory tests for those ready to embark on a spiritual path. Such tests contain lessons of knowledge.

There are also difficult tasks that the hierophant dispenses to candidates by direct or indirect assignment. In the latter, the student will have to make a decision to either succumb to the inertia of the situation or overcome these adverse

> *There is no "one-way-fits-all" path.*

circumstances and advance. Occasionally such tests offer trials of faith and ego. At that time, lust-for-result will surface and laziness will rear its omnipresent head. It is important to remember that the challenges dispensed by the teacher are never more than the aspirant can handle at that time! No one is given a greater task than he is capable of completing. Thus, those with great powers have great tasks. Those just beginning this path will be given small but significant exercise based on their level of development.

Just as a complicated violin concerto can be played by a musician who knows how to handle the instrument and read music, so it is with initiation, the receiving of knowledge. No aspir-

---

1. A reaction to something that took place, either in this life or in a past one.

ant can obtain magickal powers unless he or she is capable of receiving them and has done the preliminary work to prepare to handle them. At the time of initiation there is a noticeable and abrupt change as the initiate is opened up to special experiences in every fact of his life.

No one can provide himself his own initiatory tasks! Although the desire and potential for attainment comes from within the student, the method of contacting the Will must be taught by an Adept. There is no "one-way-fits-all" path. The divine secrets cannot be revealed until one has learned and displayed one's qualifications to the hierophant. One who attempts a method of self-initiation is doomed to failure and will not learn anything properly. (Self-help is, of course, quite different from self-initiation. It can be valuable.)

Initiation

Students who have completed the preliminary preparations and who are deemed worthy, who are seen to regularly perform their practices with quality, may be invited to undertake entrance into the Order. The aspirant must be considered valuable to the Great Work. Also, it must be evident that the aspirant can benefit from this path.

What helps a candidate to qualify? His deeds, i.e., his ability to cause change. Nice words or intentions alone are useless. The hierophant gives the candidate certain tasks and will individually guide him through a process. However, only those who truly desire to know the mysteries of the universe will complete this process.

Initiation rituals are held rarely or at regular times. The first grade of initiation is that of "probationer." Well before this formal ritual, the candidate is informed of all the ramifications of this commitment. He is told what is required of him and what he will be receiving. The details of the actual ceremony are withheld until the time of the ritual.

The candidate is given a considerable amount of time to decide whether or not he wishes to undertake this serious commitment. He is taught that initiation is a bond to certain universal forces of God that cannot be compromised.

After initiation, certain occult knowledge is revealed. The desire to do one's Will becomes more fulfilling.

The initiate's Order is his doorway to the universal forces. As a member, he will always be provided for; spirit always provides for the Magickian. Probationers are each given their own magickal motto. Embedded within these words are their early steps to attainment. It has been dictated by the higher wisdom of the Order. It is the probationer's discipline to unravel this as his Will dictates. He is also given a magickal name. All the information he receives and the work he does in the Order must be kept secret under severe occult penalty. The hierophant/priestess must divulge knowledge of powers slowly, so the risk of imprudence by the initiate is minimal. The more knowledge, the greater the responsibility. The grade of probationer mainly concerns devotion, knowledge, and perseverance for subsequent growth. The hierophant/priestess is compassionate and never issues disciplines that will demean the aspirant's Will. Although the lessons of humility and destruction of the ego may be difficult, they must be learned through experience. All this is done in love, the great cosmic law of the universe.

Life as an Initiate

Initiation is part of continuous process of evolution, along with various tasks and rewards. One starts on the bottom of the Tree and masters each sephirah up to the top. One can remain in any grade for a very long or very short time; each initiate attains at his or her own individual pace! If an initiate fails in a given discipline, he or she is simply given another task which he can hopefully complete. No one, however, is immune to falling, and just as in climbing a tree, the higher up one climbs, the harder is the fall. If someone believes he is above yielding to temptation, he can lose everything and this misused power will then haunt him!

Gaining power is simple; controlling it is difficult, but it is the essence of the path. Thus, a responsible organization teaches its initiates how to control the magickal forces slowly, gradually and thoroughly. If one abuses his knowledge, whether intentionally or not, he will find only despair or worse. This has been the downfall of many fine Magickians. As a result, casualties occur among those who don't have the experience and training to control powerful forces.

Earlier, initiation was referred to as evolution. Not only does the individual go through initiations, but so too does the whole of humanity. Man is constantly evolving, not in the Darwinian sense, but in the aspect of spiritual growth.

In man's early days he lived in greater harmony with Nature. He then progressed to where he was chosen to become Earth's ruler. The swing of the pendulum was extreme. He became so infatuated with himself that he all but forgot God, the very force that created him. Thus, we witness man worshipping man!

We have just entered into a new age which the ancient Egyptians predicted would be a resurrection of the more Godlike state of man.

Path Hopping

There are many paths to the same light; but all paths to enlightenment demand hard work. Along each path are certain requirements, and the closer one gets to the goal, the more rigorous the training.

The term path hopping refers to one who commits himself to one spiritual path than/then goes to another without fulfilling any. However, simply learning a path is different from commitment. It is the practice that one does using a specific set of energies and then abandoning it that can lead to problems.

Sometimes a student is not willing to work for his attainment. It is at this point that the rational mind might make up all sorts of "logical excuses" why one should give in and try something easier (even though it may be less rewarding.)

A path that only emphasizes philosophy touches little of the student's energy field, where the keys to the true self lay. Thus there is less training required. Conversely, a path that teaches one how to tap the powerful forces of Nature requires the ability to control such powers and demands great practice.

When you begin to practice a particular spiritual path, you develops a previously dormant energy rhythm that attracts various forces of a like kind. If you do things concurrently that are opposite to those forces, an inner conflict of these delicate vibrations will occur. Thus, before you decide to devote yourself to a particular path, you should be acquainted with it to make sure it is the right one for you.

A valid path will allow you to get acquainted with it without coercion to continue past that point. When a person mingles his auric force with a spiritual teacher, he must do so with sincere commitment rather than idle curiosity. It is the responsibility of the spiritual teacher to provide the aspirant with a thorough acquaintance of the path before he offers a commitment. Thus a thorough "courtship" between path and student is a prerequisite. To be sure of the candidate's preparedness, the teacher must know him well.

When an individual chooses a path on speculation rather than genuine insight, auric and energy dispersion problems are prevalent. One can scatter one's intellect, but scattering the battery of the life force itself (and leaving bits of it in a variety of places) is very unwise.

> *There are many paths to the same light.*

Throughout history, it has been a pattern that those who erratically jump from spiritual teacher to spiritual teacher, path to path, often end up in depravity. So think carefully before tiring of your spiritual path and trying something different. If you do try a different path, hope that your prospective teacher will see any previous links and properly decide whether or not it would benefit you to study with him.

Understand that if the prospective teacher you have chosen denies your request, it shouldn't be misunderstood or taken as an insult. It is sometimes better to reject students who would experience conflicts rather than to knowingly increase their risk of damage.

Sex and Magick

The Order that issues this material has no moral opinions. Instead, it respects the mechanics of nature and teaches the aspirant how to align himself with the natural laws of the universe he attempts to uncover and control. This is what magick is.

Here are some answers to several questions that come up during the course of study of Magick. First know that sexual Magick is a very powerful force and there

> *While promiscuity is an imbalance, so is celibacy.*

is a certain amount of the aspirant's energy being directed somewhere during the sex act. Imagine the power raised through yoga asanas or ritual, for example. Now imagine the power raised through the energy of sexual orgasm. Sexual Magick, due to its power, should not be taught until the student has leaned to control energy and has greatly attained.

While promiscuity is an imbalance, so is celibacy. However, the magickal aspirant must be very careful with whom he or she has sex. Once one has had sexual relations with a person, an aura bond is created which lasts forever. Since this aura mingling does occur, sexual relationships should only be had with someone the aspirant is willing to share his or her identity and life force with! If this partner can't be found, it is suggested that the aspirant wait until he or she is ready to be found by such a partner. Partnerships happen naturally. They can't be forced nor can they be avoided. Even though such a wait may be very difficult, it will help the aspirant learn to master the elements of the physical body. Dominion over the physical must be achieved as one is allowed to entrance into the more etherial forces. However, these attainment tasks and initiations can only be given to those who are initiated. So, learning to harness sexual power for spiritual purposes is not even a topic of discussion for the beginner, who has other things to resolve first.

So, it is with love—pledging one's love, one makes an eternal oath with all of the considerations of a true love. The power of words must be used with discretion. The bond made by an oath exists forever! Either party may cancel their performance of it on earth but its energy can never be uncreated. For one who is aware of this, the karmic repercussions of not fulfilling an oath are greater, than for one who is ignorant of it. Thus one must be fit to receive such knowledge because once one is aware of it, he becomes accountable for it.

The manifestion of sexual energy can be compared to the polarities of a battery. If performed naturally, it is very energizing; if not it weakens one just like a diffused battery runs down. This simple battery concept is based on (in a binary relationship) the dual opposites of negative and positive. All energy is similarly based. The positive/negative polarity of sex conforms to the natural laws of all energy.

The word Alchemy is misused today and has become a popular buzz word. There is a relationship between sex and magickal Alchemy. But sex in this instance implies libido, slightly different than the popular Freudian concept, i.e., the forceful energy that impels or motivates a person's energy toward an act or object. This energy can be directed only if used appropriately. It comes from something higher than your mind—a higher state which has a unique magickal purpose in your life. Therefore the mystery that the Adept unfolds is the applied purpose of this bounty. The enlightened master is the only source that the advanced practitioner can depend on to provide such accurate advice.

People ask whether celibacy, liberal sex, or puritanism is the way of the western magickal tradition. The following answer is only one method of addressing this subject.1

The guided discipline of a) harnessing physical energies and b) transmitting them into higher energies is only possible if properly learned and performed. If not, the energy raised by sex Magick might be displaced without control. This would be self destructive like the meltdown of a nuclear reactor. Or, re-

---

1. I do not condemn or pass judgement on the teachings or practices of others that may not agree with this approach . No one is in such a position to judge another's spirituality.

176

pression caused by forced celibacy, sexual trauma, transmutation mistakes, or other events, ultimately erupt in one big orgy designed to release the build up of energy, e.g., the increasing number of priests who improperly direct their libido inward and then "explore" and perform heinous perversions (not just sexual activity!) such as molesting young boys. Thus celibacy for moral code only and without proper direction is usually injurious and unhealthy, often ending in a conflictual madness. At the right time in a magickal aspirant's practices, however, celibacy is used as a bodily discipline only, another training method that will teach control over the elements.

Relationship Failures and Loneliness

Love is certainly a factor in a complete and whole life; everyone should have a mate, unless there are any karmic reasons that would prohibit it. When you work to prepare yourself as a proper lover, that is to know yourself, you know the limits and the magnitude of what you can give and receive. By the magnetism of the universe, you cannot help but attract this complimentary force.

The phenomenon of romantic breakup resulting in loneliness is rampant. There are two reasons for this distress. First, people attach themselves to another too easily and too quickly (via the emotions of infatuation and without awareness of the self). Second, people try to fill in what is missing in their life with a surrogate person. People feel infatuation, desire, enjoyment, companionship, physical attraction, etc. for another person and mistake these emotions as love or else redefine the term love so that it will encompass these above mentioned feelings. However, the magickal concept of love is a monogamous union for the duration of your partner's life in which you are perpetually desirous, considerate, and wanting to satisfy that person. So dating someone, liking and enjoying them is fine, but do you want to spend the rest of your life with that person? Can you enjoy serving that person and having him or her serve you?

To say "I love you," means I devote and share my most caring feeling of life with you, desiring all of your most caring feelings of life. However, to give devotion does not mean to give up one's identity (the Will). Love is not surrendering your own true Will, or expecting that of your partner. Instead, it is enjoying each other's energy as individuals to harmonize like two pieces of a puzzle fitting together exactly. If not, something is missing.

How many times have you seen people get married and, shortly thereafter, age quickly, lose their desire for the things they used to enjoy, become attached to and adopt their partner's desires, sacrificing their own identities? Next thing you know, you haven't seen them for a few years, perhaps they have a child, they are both overweight, getting along alright with each other but only "getting by," having lost their previous interests, mistakenly believing they are required to deny their own Will's for their partners sake.

To identify love, the word love should not be used superficially. It's not that you are restricted from loving more than one person; it's that infatuation would probably be mistaken for your Will when you match yourself with several people. Thus you must approach the possibility of love as completely as you possibly can with another. There may be times that you will believe you are in love and then find out that you were wrong. The universe allows people to learn from their

> *It is the magickal opinion that the word hate should be totally discarded.*

mistakes. This is directed more so to people who overuse the word love without knowing its implications. How many times do you use the word love? I love this salad, I love this idea, I love that artist, I loved that book, I love to sleep. A good exercise would be to replace the word love with enjoy, get satisfaction from, etc. and reserve the word love for special (appropriate) occasions. It is the magickal opinion that the word hate should be totally discarded; if one has good self control it should never be used.

There are ways to prevent relationship failures. It is important to ask yourself what you need. What are you getting? What can you give? What do you feel? What do you not feel with a partner?

Introspection into the true Will will reveal your purpose and how your partner can fit in with that purpose. Finding an appropriate mate requires knowing your true self. How can you attract the forces to fulfill you if you do not know yourself? This is a long and arduous process. Through magickal study one does get to know the true self, and, once that happens, will automatically recognize the mate that will synchronize with their true self, and their mate will feel the same synchronization.

When people connect with the wrong people, and their relationships ultimately end in failure, they want to know why. It's not because they didn't look deep enough into the other person, but because they didn't look deep enough into themselves. To find your true partner, first find yourself. If you cannot be happy with yourself and you need someone else to do this for you, you do not know yourself. This spells failure for a relationship or no relationship at all.

The independent person is not dependent upon external circumstances or other people for gratification or satisfaction. He will revel not egotistically but joyously in his own actions. If he is unhappy he will search for the reason and correct it, not look for someone to "make it better."

To become a fit receptacle for love, learn that you are part of everything that has ever been made manifest. This unity with creation is also called love but it is love of a higher nature.[1] It is a true ecstasy that will fill you so completely that you will not depend on any other person or thing to bring joy to your life.

What is missing?

Very often the lover who gets hurt in a relationship has settled for a partner who appears to be able to provide something that is missing in himself and demands further that the partner provide him with a joyous state that he is lacking.

If you are not able to control yourself and your emotions, how can you expect another person to do that for you? Even if he could, it would weaken your Will and your soul because the manipulation of one person by another is unproductive and destructive. There is a rush of excitement and a fear of loss that most people feel when they fall in love. When they try to hold on to the loved one often the relationship will painfully fall apart.

Now you know how to prevent a failed relationship, but how do you cope with the pain of a relationship that has already fallen apart? The most effective way is to identify who you are, to realize you have an inner joy which the process of enlightenment can bring out. Some call it *samadhi*, some call it attainment, some call it perfection. When you are in such a state, you

1. See Chesed (Qabalah)

infuse yourself with spirit and pull out and rectify the destructive parts of yourself leaving only the constructive parts. This helps to ease the pain that one unnecessarily goes through because one chose the wrong partner. You must develop yourself, hold on to yourself, and remember that doing your Will is what you truly desire and putting that person before your own higher self causes pain when that person is no longer there. This is not to say that egocentricity is necessary! The more you know yourself and your Will, the more harmony you develop using this higher state called your true identity.

A broken relationship is the symbol of a life of illusion. When both partners know and understand reality, a relationship cannot fail! But most people settle for a poor relationship as a cure for something else. Instead, learn to go deep inside and get to know the true self that was ignored in a painful relationship where you placed the partner on a pedestal giving all your attention to them instead of towards your own self-growth. Such a great attachment to another person's Will, and such a great detachment from you own Will and identity is a state of disease and will only lead to pain. Learn more about yourself and look towards uniting that hidden perception of yourself. Shed your ego, your self-image, and see what is truly inside, which is part of a powerful divine creation with the power of sadness or joy, the power to destroy or build. The feeling that comes about with spiritual attainment will allow you to put your mate in proper perspective with your true Will. To lose a mate is painful, but to lose yourself is much more devastating. By whatever name it is called, you must learn to "know thyself."

Why Spiritual Groups Succeed or Fail

A certain dynamic occurs in a true magickal Order, that makes the Order or group great or, in the worst instances, causes its decay. This has been seen throughout the history of some very fine but uncontrolled Orders.

The true initiate gives up the idea that his or her relationships with others in the Order are either social or superficial. There is no need for the false dialogue that would normally go on between people in a social situation. Instead, initiates share a much deeper spiritual relationship (even though very separately) on a sublime level.

This sharing of a common force is like many cells operating together to make up a human body. This link is established by initiation. Each Order has its own characteristic energy.

Unbeknownst to the members of the Order, but visible to the authority, when good fortune befalls one member, it befalls all, but manifests in different ways. Conversely, when one member experiences ill fortune of any kind, the repercussions effect all members. This is always the case, and often at least one member observes this.

Therefore, every member is responsible not only to himself for his acts, thoughts, etc., but to the whole group. There is no escaping this phenomenon of nature. Your actions will effect every other member of the group, just as the heart does not act alone, but affects all the other organs of the body.

Thus, a candidate is invited to undertake the serious and unbreakable bond of initiation only if the hierophant believes his words, thoughts, actions, etc. will not vary greatly from the groups goals. The obligation is great, for when the initiate acts, it is never alone! The results of any members's expression of denial of self-improvement effects the entire group. One frustrated member will spread this vibration to all the others. It will take its tool on the weak ones, and the originator of this force must bear a heavy karma. On the other hand, one member who holds up his end and conquers the demons of the lower self, as gradual as it may be, fortifies all the members, assisting them in trying to do the same.

Fortunately, the hierophant is powerful enough to help, assuming the others are industrious and sincere about their climb. As leader, he provides the opportunity to enter and partake of the Order's knowledge and resources. The aspirant will either use or misuse them. Nature will then respond accordingly, often in the least expected ways. This concept, like all magickal concepts, is simple. However, it is probably the most important one for initiates to know.

Adjusting to the Changing Times

We have been witness to the prophecies as signposts of nature's timetable. We saw the famous Nostradamus precisely describe the rise to power of Adolph Hitler. We saw a more low-profiled "Fulcanelli" warn the American government not to develop nuclear bombs "for public use." When he revealed how these bombs could rule the world[1], and the most confidential atomic equations, every government on the face of the earth searched for this still anonymous man. We saw a plethora of prophets warn of the financial collapse of a nation, called "the depression." (It was astrologically blatant). We saw, not that many years ago, many not-so-famous prophets forecast a deadly disease that would rise enormously at this time: A.I.D.S. We saw Edgar Cayce predict the forced fluoridation of public waters, killing marine and animal life and proven to have claimed innumerable human victims. (It is added at eight times the human toxicity level!)

> *Nature doesn't discriminate.*

Just recently many natural disasters and other changes have been occurring in increasing number and frequency. These are personal and immediate changes that *directly* affect *your* life as you read this! The ancient ones said that these times would occur. How should you prepare?

First devote the time to understand how prophecy and preparation work. Then you will be able to act. If you avoid putting in such time and energy, you'll get back just as much as a result.

Nature doesn't discriminate. So good intentions, awareness, etc. doesn't exempt you from the awesome forces of the universe. If your intent is to help someone by plugging in a lamp so they can read, and you happen to be standing in a

---

1. If you accept that man, the founder of atomic fission, is threatened and oppressed by it instead of liberated by it. (When was the last time you used you cyclotron "to serve you better"?)

puddle of water, nature will electrocute you. It won't change its laws for you!

Certain change is immanent to the Creation. "Change is stability," said Aleister Crowley. (If the planets don't change position our system will implode into the sun.)

Wisdom is not knowledge; in adapting to this most profound time of change you can chose to either a) adhere to the forces of nature, Spirit, God, Universal Consciousness (or whatever you want to label "It") or b)chose to resists "It" by any deceptive reason or rationale.

The Creator's tools of *personal* understanding which specifically harmonize you with this new aeon, are for the wise. The misuse or denial of one's own higher self cannot make a person a fit receiver for such knowledge. Prophesies (Nostradamus, Revelations, Chaldean Oracles, Pyramids, etc.) appear cryptic or inaccurate to persons who are closed or unprepared. True spirituality provides experience that liberates. Thus, it prepares the person for the coming time.

This aeon consists of the collection of unique individuals performing the "alchemy" of assisting nature, as mankind is the governing species of the planet. If each individual learns to attain to his own true Will, this civilization will be man's "Golden Age." The forces that rule this aeon require that every person chose his circumstances rather than have circumstances choose him. Indecisiveness cannot exist in this new aeon. The fear of making a decision no longer fits into this scheme of nature.

That which each person causes will reflect back to him or her. Thus, today's prophesies include:

Food shortages.

Drastic water shortages.

Daily (literally) earthquakes.

Volcanoes.

Pole shifts.

Magnetic field changes (already drastically decreased).

Other erratic global changes.

Major cites decaying.

War.

Man's possessiveness and greed causing mass economic
    failure.

Reappearance of antiquated diseases.

These are simply nature's responses to the "old aeon man." To resist this new aeon will inhibit your transition from the old one into the present.

To prepare for these changing energies, learn to experience the self through arduous training and observe the change that authentic spirituality causes in your life. For the privilege of contacting the force which created you, know "you" first. The Creator will not beg you to come to It. You have to make that choice.

The First Step of the Path

W here do these ancient teachings lead to? They lead to the beginning of your spiritual quest. You must go to the root in order to begin your start upon the Tree of Life. Additionally, Magick is practiced as simultaneous—not isolated—disciplines. All areas of your life are related and none are independent.

You chose your birth to do your Will during this incarnation. Thus it is said Magick is the discovery of your True Will. Therefore, every particle of your life has an effect on you and therefore your *whole life* is Magick as you choose it! Magick is life, growth, death and life again. Just when one thinks he or she has found the "end" (the culmination of applied magickal abilities), he or she realizes it is only the beginning towards the entire process! The serpent with its tail in its mouth (called the *auroborous*) reminds the student of this. The student also realizes that Magick is not the goal but the method or tool which can bring him or her to the goal, whether it be on the grand scale in day-to-day life.

The experience that goes along with magickal understanding transforms the soul. This is how Magick works. Thus to be a Magickian (one who Magick as one's path toward God) is to grasp the concepts. However, the details of knowledge of the precepts means nothing. A much more valuable knowledge is of the "self" which will dissolve and reveal the innner, created and native reflection of the Creator on a greater scale. In other words, while you are not God, your soul, which has been covered by exterior influences, is the real "you" as created by God and not as intellectualized by your mind. Although even the slightest of the popular "systems" may make you aware of "spirit," true magickal experience is the necessity for uniting with the occult forces of Creation! Furthermore, while data and inspiration are fine, they cannot replace the magickal forces derived from the experiences of an Adept who has crossed that bridge to sacred attainment.

Attainment is *not* the mastery of the magickal tool. It is the result caused by the precise utilization of that tool. Thus the tool of intuition or psychism must never be mistaken for attainment! This would surely lead the seeker into dismal failure. In Magick, the student receives the powers of the gods, not of the Hierophant, who only brings him to them.

The process is individually designed by the Hierophant for every student the teacher chooses to take on. (In a following book, I hope to go deeper, and explain in detail the four virtues of an Adept: to Will, to Dare, to Know, to Be Silent.) The guidelines of the Western Mystery Tradition are the Laws of Nature (the Universe...God). In our Hermetic Magick, the "design" is to become an adequate receptacle to receive those forces. It is not good to invoke those forces without preparing oneself to handle them.

You chose your birth to do your Will during this incarnation.

The concepts explained in this book are those that the Adept teaches the student in certain ways, dispensing them to the student in specific practices. The Adept teaches the ways to invoke such energies according to the ability of the student to receive them. Otherwise they would bypass the student and have been called forth for naught. Although God is within man, we must learn that God manifests as things that appear "mundane" to us, God's creation. Thus, take everything as an act of God for the purpose of Karma or of exercising and testing your progress (even though you may not think so at the time.) Thus, the Magick taught at the Winged Disk is both profound and formal—and yet as the same time simple and on a practical level.

Magick is not a religion. Magick is the harnessing of forces of Nature and therefore uniting with them in the process. Religion is the study, adoration, and belief of and in an event and in the symbology of that primal event. Yet every religion is founded upon Magick. Even the most anti-magickal religions of today base their beliefs upon magickal events (often called and accepted as "miracles," i.e., the supernatural).

Exactly what are the concepts of Magick anyway? The ancient Romances called the high winds "Jupiter." This phenomenon was considered a god, but such winds have God as a source anyway. Although science has analyzed and understands such winds, does this understanding make these torrents less than God? Should we discount this phenomenon just because we know, to a degree, how the form? Cannot we still consider this phenomenon as Nature (God)? Should we discount the deeper, esoteric value of something just because we can "explain" it? To do so would not only bring down the institutions of the occult but would also destroy the fables of established religion.

There are several types of Magick. The Magick in this book centers upon the development of the self rather than the reconstruction of society. Coercion towards any single path is considered evil, as it may prevent you from embarking upon another path which is your particular way toward God.

How do you know Magick actually works, if you were to study it? What "proof" can God give you?

A long time ago, a student was told not to use much water from his well because it was prophecized that his well was going dry. He was warned he's run out of water if he wasn't prudent. Of course he had to follow his master's instruction, even though he seemed to have plenty of water for his needs.

A week later, he went to his teacher and asked if he could be relieved from his water rationing and go back to full use of water. His teacher denied his request. This went on weekly for quite some time. Finally his teacher consented to his request to be free with his water. A week later, the student triumphantly said to the teacher, "I told you I wouldn't run out of water!"

The question that remains unanswered is, "Was the Magick in the observation of the teacher or was it in the preservation of the student?"

The answer is, "Who knows, who cares, why bother?"

Actually the student caused the Magick of free-flowing waters by allocation. Was this any less a magickal weapon than the accoutrements and names on his altar? Magick comes in many forms. Explanation is useless in the quest for the magickal life. What one *does* is one's Magick! The reason doesn't matter. Contemplate on Magick and on Reason.

Yet another reason for one to prepare oneself for a magickal life are the ancient prophets and prophecies of the Winged Disk. Many of the prophecies have already taken place and will continue in their clarity as time goes on. Those who are wise will heed them. Those who are ignorant will choose to ignore them. This has been so in so many previous cultures. Even the residents of the advanced civilization of Atlantis were given warnings of an abrupt change for over a generation.

The prophecies of the Winged Disk that have already occurred are irrelevant now. The specifics of the future are important, but this book is not meant for that topic. So here is a general outline of what to look for. Note today's date and mark them down as they continue to occur.

Magnetism will be the new technology.

Briefly, the years 1999, 2000, 2001, 2002, 2012 and 2021 will be paramount. At that time, the golden age of man's rebuilding will occur. Instead of building statues in parks, of soldiers on horses, statues will be built of gods. We already see the demise of many large instituons—ones that man never thought could fall!

Natural disasters, including (before the year 2001) a meteorite/asteroid, will devastate the planet and its future climate. Mount Ranier will explode. Niagara Falls will cease to exist. Electricity dependent upon such waterfalls will fail, throwing cities into panic. Mexico City is one warning signpost. More major earthquakes will signal cataclysmic events on all levels, throughout the world. After California sinks, Manhattan will follow, but not immediately. The animal kingdom will rebel as a group. After several large accidents, mankind will discover that nuclear energy is a curse and will abandon it. Magnetism will be the new technology. Computers will be totally eliminated long before 2012. Gradually man will go back to pencils and manilla file folders. This will begin at about 2001.

Severe problems will render major drinking-water sources unusable in one day! By the year 2000, there will be water battles, making petroleum commodities bottom out, as oil will become a thing of the past. The cost of water will be far more than oil. Burglars will no longer break in to steal your television and VCR but will go for your food and water.

As governments encourage social unrest, in a worldwide conspiracy, they will use such unrest as an excuse to regulate or ban most rights, such as travel within and without a country. Also, in one day, they will disallow the practice of all religions except for the Big Three. Militia breaking down your doors will be commonplace—for "reasons of national security." Tanks routinely will caravan down the streets to maintain the "state of order." In fact governments will be forced to put politics aside and ban together for survival. But before that, by 2001, the two top countries will no longer accept coexistence. Battle will ensue for the "top prize."

As disease and other natural disasters occur, mass burials, using bulldozers, will occur. (The film *Things to Come* is an excellent depiction of what it will be like.)

Like all the other destroyed civilizations, signs will be given and have been given: red moons: near-Earth asteroids; political, social and business changes; technological threats; increased earthquakes. Even though the number of severe quakes (over 5 on the Richter scale) has tripled in less than ten years, the newspapers bury this information in the back pages, right next to the used tire ads. Even when 7.5 quakes occur regularly, the papers claim that the only damage done was "Ma Kettle's favorite plate fell off the wall and broke." In the 1970s, 7.5 earthquakes were almost unheard of!

Money will still be used but be nearly worthless. In fact, no investment will be stable.

After a third of the population perishes in a few short years, the survival of mankind will be at stake. We will have been beaten to our knees. All of this is a natural reaction to mankind's actions. Man charges the energy of the aethyr and earth more than you think. True Science (Nature) will rebel, not intelligently but instinctively.

Salvation is like attainment. It is individual. If you are ready to dispense with those things which are not in harmony with the Laws of Nature (and this does not mean sleeping on straw mats) you will survive. If you do not see these signs over the years, you will fail miserably and perish. Each of you is what you make of yourself.

This devastation is only a cleaning process, to clear away the old. It's happened before and will happen again. Call it man's reincarnation, if you will. Those in harmony with the laws will thrive to bring in the new aeon. This will be man's Golden Age, where peace, beauty, harmony and exhaltation shall occur.

So we see that the Magick of this 2155-year aeon is different than that of the past aeon. In this age, every soul must make his or her choice. You cannot continue to fence-sit and ask, "What will it be? What will it be?" Man has the power to reason that is unique. No animal has it. Thus every person must individually decide for him- or herself how to prepare for self-development at this time.

Certainly there will be those who will have beliefs and philosophies which disagree with our practices. The teachings herein contained represent only the Great White Brotherhood. That Brotherhood is the "body" of all such esoteric teachings. It is not a formal association of all esoteric paths. However, the energy collectively created by similar paths generates a force which attracts yet more energy. Which is how the new aeon will grow. No true spiritual path seeks expansion of its membership. In this aeon, in which every individual has their own unique initiations, every man and woman can do their Will. The human race is ready and is under the guidance of the god of this aeon. In the past, man had to develop the stability that would allow him to recognize true mystical experience for himself. To thrust imperceivable experiences upon the "child" would have been detrimental towards appreciating his individuality.

But one is made up of more than his or her known "identity." As a matter of fact, one is *not* one's known identity! You are an identity emitted by God, as part of God's creation. So when you say "I," does that mean "I" the employee, son/daughter/friend, neighbor, mate, etc.? There are the multitudes of identities that one assumes in life! The Magickian has found his or her one true identity (which is made up of many unrestricted endeavors). At the same time the Magickian manifests the true identity, he or she harmonizes with the circumstances that his or her nature puts him- or herself into. Thus he or she is able to undertake any and every situation.

The "I" is more than your face or your name, or the image that others have of you. It is even more than you perceive yourself to be. That is, it is more than the tangible physical body you call "I." The body changes during and after the lifetime. The intellect and "handling of emotion" does too. But the one thing that remains consistent and it immortal is the true "I" in its native God-created form. The goal of the aspirant is to pierce the coverings of that native "I."

This is the age of Aquarius during which will be the culmination of one's capacity. In other terms, it is also the aeon of Horus, the matured and fully perfected "god" who grew from just an innocent child (called Harpocrates).

In this book, you have been given a general encounter to the beginning practices of the magickal student. You have started a current of energy that will attract its similar energy. Many people who read this book "coincidentally" encounter a teacher or other ways to this path. That is how Nature works: Like attracts like.

> *The human race is ready and is under the guidance of the god of this aeon.*

By your reading of this book, you have started a current of magnetic energy that will attract similar energy towards you, a little at a time, via "coincidences." Thus you may be led to further perusal of Magick or, at least, discover the mysteries of Magick within your present path. Obviously you bought this book because you are a seeker. However, it is not intended to change your spiritual path but can perhaps add a more significant dimension to it.

Thus the *Teachings of the Winged Disk* has taken you on a journey upon a path toward that end. It has preserved the topics included in the curriculum of candidates along this ancient path. (The specifics are reserved for them only, however.) This is how our tradition is passed along from generation to generation, century to century. While the lay person will comprehend it, the wise man will discover the teachings of our Order by his ability to "read between the lines" and he will be fully versed in "cosmic" terms and authority. So it is with every holy text. While the lay people take them literally, the wise ones understand their hidden meaning, formulae, and practices. Perhaps a subsequent *Teachings of the Winged Disk* will be in order in the future, the inferences to the New Aeon made in the *Teachings of the Winged Disk* are another whole book. There is a tremendous amount of knowledge to be shared. (The Academy previously published some of its teachings in six other booklets, which comprise *The Practica Arcanum.* So *Teachings of the Winged Disk* might be considered to comprise the Academy's seventh book in a series of books.)

Savor and reread every sentence of *Teachings of the Winged Disk* because it was written as a process to open you up. As you read, remember the cardinal rule: never to force that which you are not ready to comprehend. This book contains age-old teachings that have been verbally passed down through the millennia. Although the Holy Order of the Winged Disk does not have open membership, it does have an "outer" contact, the International Academy of Hermetic Knowledge. It teaches the starting specifics accessible to nearly every person seeking this type of enlightenment. It is the precursor to possibilities of future, deeper study. Readers interested in probing deeper into the mysteries may write to the Academy for information:

International Academy of Hermetic Knowledge
P. O. Box 4384
2150 Wise Street
Charlottesville, VA 22905

About the Author

Phaedron∴ is the Hierophant of the Holy Order of The Winged Disk, an old magickal organization dedicated to hermetic, qabalistic, gnostic, rosicrucian, and alchemical practices.

The Order keeps a very low profile. Its teachings have been traditionally passed verbally from Adept to initiate. More than a decade ago, it became necessary to slightly raise its veil to provide greater accessibility for those to find such a spiritual path when they are ready, as spirit designs.

The Winged Disk does not follow the teachings of any one person. It recognizes that there is a seed of truth in every tradition. Its teachings are not for those who want self-aggrandizement. Although it may be compared to such Orders as the Golden Dawn, etc. The Winged Disk is completely autonomous, independent and not connected with any other spiritual group. (The International Academy of Hermetic Knowledge is, however, an organ of The Winged Disk). The *Teachings of the Winged Disk* is a compilation of material issued annually by the Order from 1987 through 1990, that has been edited, and added to.

In March of 1991, The Winged Disk founded The International Academy of Hermetic Knowledge, an independent home study program offering the techniques of western magick, spiritual practice and special guidance not available in any books. Phaedron is named as its director.

Phaedron∴ teaches privately, counsels spiritually, and holds small group classes in ritual magick and related esoteric methods. He implements the Order's philosophy of approaching the subject in a thorough, safe and realistic manner. As an Adept, he receives sincere seekers.

Phaedron∴ has been a guest on several nationwide television and radio shows, as well as the subject of filmed productions and newspaper and magazine articles only for the purpose of exemplifying a true and healthy image of white Magick.

ceachings of
the winged disk

This book is to be considered volume IX of *The Practica Arcanum*, authorized by the Winged Disk. It is a completely rewritten and amended compilation of *The Practica Arcanum* volumes I, II, and IV.

Volume III is a set of two audio tapes which are not available

Volume V consists of twelve *Monographs*, giving specific instructions and techniques. It may be obtained from the Academy.

Volume VI is the *Nineteen Dictums*, issued privately and restricted to certain select members of the Order only!

Volume VII is the set of *Apprentice Monographs*, available from the Academy.

VIII consists of the set of *Mysteries of the Temple*, also available from the Academy.

International Acdemy of Hermetic Knowledge
P.O. Box 4384
2150 Wise Street
Charlottesville, VA 22905

"Deadlytown"

—by Nancy Ziegler

The amazing true story of one of the most haunted places in America!

Fascinated by the history of Dudleytown, Connecticut, paranormal investigators Nancy Ziegler and her husband Robin are obsessed with discovering the truth about this abandoned town. Located in the appalacian mountains, the inhabitants of Dudleytown either went mad, committed suicide, disappeared, or lost everything they hold dear.

Each expidition to dudleytown produced paranormal activity that affected Nancy, her husband and their guests—and was often captured on film! sometimes the evil spirits followed them home! Eventually the obsession with dudleytown leads to disaster.

Deadlytown is a chilling account of the supernatural. It is heavily illustrated with photographs showing ghost lights, strange balls of energy, mists, and apperations.

Upcoming From Belfry Books!

Belfry Books, A division of Toad Hall, Inc.
Rural Route 2 Box 16-B
Laceyville, PA 18623
FAX 717 869-1031

Technical Notes: Production design by Steven Dale Birch. This book was designed on a Mactintosh™ Quadra 630, using a UMAX™ Vista S8 scanner and a DELTIS™ Olympus external optical drive. All graphics were manipulated in Adobe™ Photoshop,text and page laypout was done in PageMaker®. Body copy is ITC Cheltenham Book.

Steven's print media servies can be reached at:
23420 Happy Valley Dr.
Newhall, CA 91321
FAX: 805 288-1754